ACKNOWLEDGMENTS

Solution Tree Press would like to thank the following reviewers:

Edward Callahan
History Teacher and IB Coordinator
Florence High School
Florence, Arizona

Melissa Cartwright
Seventh- and Eighth-Grade Teacher
Helper Middle School
Helper, Utah

Teresa Dobler
Science Teacher
Washington Latin Public Charter School
Washington, DC

Tami Ewell
Language Arts Teacher
Copper Mountain Middle School
Herriman, Utah

Cassie Hetzel
Fifth-Grade Teacher
Thermopolis Middle School
Thermopolis, Wyoming

Maria Krum
Special Education and Mathematics Teacher
Valencia Middle School
Los Lunas, New Mexico

Nicole McRee
Science Instructional Coach
Kildeer Countryside District #96
Buffalo Grove, Illinois

Jon Moore
English Teacher
Shepherd High School
Shepherd, Montana

Visit **go.SolutionTree.com/21stcenturyskills** to download the free reproducibles in this book.

TABLE OF CONTENTS

About the Author xi

Foreword xiii

Introduction 1

PART ONE

Understanding New Needs and a New Approach for a Digital Generation 5

CHAPTER 1

The New Needs of a Changing Generation 7

The Situation in Schools 8
The Problems for Students 11
Conclusion 14
Questions for Discussion 14

CHAPTER 2

The Thinking and Processing Skills Students Need for the Future 15

The Key to Thinking in the Future—Three-Dimensional Thinking 17
The Seven Pillars of Success 19
Conclusion 28
Questions for Discussion 28

CHAPTER 3

The Key to a New Approach 29

The Curriculum as a Problem to Be Solved 30
Authentic Teaching and Assessment 32

Conclusion 35
Questions for Discussion 35

PART TWO

Learning How to Create Problems-First Projects 37

CHAPTER 4
Envision a New Role for the Teacher 39
A Critical New Role 39
A Goal for Every Subject Area 40
A Response to Resistance 41
Conclusion 41
Questions for Discussion 41

CHAPTER 5
Ensure That Problems Are First and Teaching Is Second 43
What the Problems-First Approach Looks Like 44
Benefits of the Problems-First Approach 46
Conclusion 47
Questions for Discussion 48

CHAPTER 6
Establish a Real-World Link Using Role-Play 49
Benefits of Role-Play in the Problems-First Approach 49
An Example of Role-Play in the Problems-First Approach 51
Starting Small 52
Conclusion 53
Questions for Discussion 53

CHAPTER 7
Equip Students With the Four Ds of Problem Solving .. 55
Define 56
Design 59
Do 64
Debrief 66

Conclusion 68
Questions for Discussion 69

CHAPTER 8
Expand Your View of the Curriculum 71
An Alternative to Compartmentalizing 71
A Goal of Open-Ended Problems With Unknown Possibilities 72
An Example of a Collaborative, Multisubject
Problems-First Project 73
Reaching Out 74
Finding Common Ground 74
Conclusion 74
Questions for Discussion 75

CHAPTER 9
Elevate the Students' Level of Thought 77
The Elements of Higher-Level Thinking 78
The Problem of Unreliable Data 79
The Five Steps of Information Analysis 80
The Three Aspects of Information Synthesis 82
The Importance of Information Evaluation 83
Examples of Higher-Level Thinking Within Problems-First Projects . . 84
Conclusion 87
Questions for Discussion 87

CHAPTER 10
Educate the Whole Mind 89
Encourage Fact-Based Imagination 90
Teach the Entire Writing Process 92
Enter the Idea-Storm Think Tank 94
Conclusion 98
Questions for Discussion 98

CHAPTER 11
Evaluate Holistically 99
Authentic Assessment 100
Formative Assessment and Rubrics 107
Self-Assessment as a Tool for Assessing Internal Attitude Skills . . . 108

    Conclusion 110

    Questions for Discussion 110

CHAPTER 12
Ease Yourself Out of the Picture 111

    Conclusion 112

    Questions for Discussion 113

PART THREE

Making the Shift to Problems-First Teaching 115

CHAPTER 13
Pointers for Shifting to a Problems-First Approach ... 117

    Things to Remember When Beginning Problems-First Teaching 117

    A Process for Designing Problems-First Projects 119

    The Goal of Complex Problem Solving 125

    One Project Per Term 126

    Conclusion 127

    Questions for Discussion 127

CHAPTER 14
Examples of Problems-First Lesson Plans 129

    An Example of a Problems-First Project Plan for a Junior High School Science Class 129

    An Example of a Problems-First Project Plan for a Middle School English Language Arts Class 134

    An Example of a Problems-First Project Plan for a Junior High School Social Studies Class 138

    Conclusion 144

    Questions for Discussion 145

References and Resources 147

Index 153

ABOUT THE AUTHOR

Ted McCain, first and foremost, is an educator who has taught high school students at Maple Ridge Secondary School in British Columbia, Canada, since the 1980s. Although he has had several opportunities to take other jobs, both inside education and in the private sector, he has felt his primary calling is to prepare teenagers for success as they move into adult life. He is the coordinator of Digital Arts Academy for the Maple Ridge School District in Vancouver, British Columbia, and has taught computer networking, graphic design, and desktop publishing for Okanagan University.

In 1997, Ted received the Prime Minister's Award for Teaching Excellence. Ted received this prestigious Canadian national award for his work in developing a real-world technology curriculum for grade 11 and grade 12 students that prepares them for postgraduation employment in website design and computer networking. The Prime Minister's Award for Teaching Excellence recognized Ted's work in creating his innovative problems-first teaching strategy, his four Ds approach to solving problems, his unique use of role playing in the classroom, and his idea of progressive withdrawal as a way to foster independence in his students. Ted has written or co-written fourteen books on the future, effective teaching strategies, educational technology, and graphic design.

Prior to entering the teaching profession, Ted worked for several years in the computer industry as a programmer, salesperson, and consultant. In addition to his work as a teacher, Ted has also consulted with school districts and businesses since the 1980s on effective teaching for the digital generation and the implementation of instructional technology. His clients have included Apple, Microsoft, Aldus, and Toyota, as well as many school districts and educational associations in Canada, the United States, Mexico, Australia, and China.

To book Ted McCain for professional development, contact pd@SolutionTree.com.

FOREWORD

Why did you become an educator? Perhaps you had a good experience in school and wanted to recreate that for others. Perhaps you wanted to share your love of your subject with students. Perhaps you were interested in how learning takes place and wanted to observe it up close. I was fascinated with the idea that small children stayed engaged in learning for what seemed like a long time. In Montessori education, the design of the physical materials in the classroom encourages students to explore while they are often unconsciously learning. For example, the binomial and trinomial cubes are three-dimensional puzzles that allow young students to experience the binomial $(a + b + c)^2$ and trinomial $(a + b + c)^3$ theorems in a physical way, long before they would be expected to learn and understand these ideas in the abstract. A box of cut-out alphabet letters allows students to share their ideas by manipulating physical letters to make words before they can securely hold a pencil and write on paper. Writing comes before reading because what an individual has to say (my story) takes precedence over what someone else has to say (the reading book). Asking about what letters make up sounds as a child writes with the moveable alphabet leads to reading.

The Montessori idea of "follow the child" affirms the importance of children taking responsibility for their own learning. The role of the teacher is to act as a liaison between the child and the learning environment. It is all about respect as well as carefully planned materials and interactions that encourage exploration, curiosity, and understanding. Through the years, as I worked with preschool children, with elementary students, and in professional development with teachers spanning kindergarten through high school, these qualities remained extremely important.

My first encounters with Ted McCain came many years ago at educational technology conferences where we were both presenting on topics such as effective technology use, project-based learning, information literacy, asking good questions, critical thinking, and creating environments where trust, collaboration, compassion, and empathy provide the foundation for deep learning. Our discussions still center on these ideas, and *Problems-First Learning: A Framework for Engaging Minds and Nurturing Thinkers in Grades 6–12* is a beautiful manifestation of Ted's deep thinking about his practice and how to make teaching and learning most effective for him and his students. Ted's book shares not only his interests in becoming an educator but also his reflections on why his practices weren't working. He was able to move past feelings of defeat when he saw his students weren't engaged in their work and didn't seem to retain what he had carefully helped them learn. He started to look at ways to engage students in meaningful projects that still required them to learn the content of his field, but within their own ways and for their own reasons. Then he spent years in implementing change in his practices, reacting to student responses, and refining what he was doing—and he still relies on feedback from students and his own reflections and observations to make his practice more relevant and effective.

We often see books in the field of education that tell us what we should be doing and why we should be doing it, but *how* isn't always so clear. Many of these books do have the students at heart—wanting to offer them a relevant, engaging experience in the classroom as well as providing skills that will stand them in good stead throughout their lives, such as critical thinking, collaboration, global understanding, and compassion. Of course, there are bodies of knowledge that every educated person needs to know that speak to being successful in life: how to read; how to communicate through written and spoken words; how to do basic math; lessons from history; how government works; skill in movement; expression through art. We also know the value of being able to plan, work together, produce a product, and reflect on our own process. Ted describes the problem-solving process as the four Ds: define, design, do, and debrief. This becomes an iterative process, which leads to going deeper in understanding on any topic through reflection.

Learning to ask good questions is often neglected in our teaching. However, it is the cornerstone of critical thinking. Early on, when the Right Question Institute (rightquestion.org) founders offered to help immigrants find out what they needed to know when talking to health professionals or their children's teachers, they created what they thought were relevant questions for their clients. Quickly they learned that confidence and power came from teaching their clients how to think about and formulate their own questions. The process that Ted describes in his book addresses this important issue head-on. If we teach students to explore their own paths into an area of study by means of a problem presented by the teacher, we can help them move from gathering information, even knowing something about the information, to really understanding and making it their own. An important part of this whole process is analyzing information, determining sources and their efficacy, and thus understanding when and where to trust what they see, read, and hear from all sources.

The "what" and "why" of educational practices are important, yet the "how" is paramount. Ted's book provides blueprints, maps, scenarios, sample lessons, and much more for changing practice to become more effective for students and teachers, including holistic assessment of student work. Change is rarely easy, but with encouragement and a good goal in mind, the result is worth the struggle. Ted's assurance through his own experience offers such a path. He suggests specific steps for starting small, understanding that anything new can be uncomfortable, and trusting that the positive effects on student learning—and on our own teaching practice—will outweigh any discomforts. Let's get started!

Sara Armstrong, PhD
Berkeley, California, USA
November 1, 2020

INTRODUCTION

I entered the teaching profession in the 1980s with high hopes of making a positive difference in the lives of my students. In my teacher training at university, I was given plentiful guidance on how to plan lessons and create assignments that would reinforce the desired learning, but very little about how to give instruction to a class. When I stood in front of a class for the first time, I did what I had seen all my teachers do when I was a student—I talked. And when I had finished talking, I gave the students a test. I didn't stop to think about why I taught this way; it just came naturally to me. The feedback that I received from my professors and my sponsor teachers affirmed that I was on the right track.

As a new teacher, the more course content I encountered in the curriculum guides, the more I talked and tested. Having students complete tests seemed like the most solid way to evaluate whether they could demonstrate that they had memorized the facts and procedures I presented to them or that they found in the textbook. Observing my more experienced colleagues teaching their classes in this way made me comfortable with teaching my own classes the same way. It was apparent to me that lecturing then testing was the way that teaching is done.

My conception of effective teaching changed, but gradually, and only after several years. I began to notice that students were forgetting what I had taught them shortly after I presented them with the material. They even forgot material they had answered correctly on recent tests. They were not able to transfer the skills I taught them to the new tasks I gave them to do, and they quickly became lost when they encountered problems that were even slightly different from those I had previously assigned. Instead of drawing from their own skill bases, students depended on me to provide them with strategies for solving new problems. I had to face the reality that my instruction was far less effective than I had hoped it would be.

The real dagger to my heart came when I realized not only that my students forget what I taught, but also that my teaching was not *engaging* them even in moments of active instruction. They were uninterested in what I had to say. My desire was to teach in a relevant, interesting manner to get my students ready for the challenges they would face in life. Instead I was giving my students the same kind of teaching I had received in school, which had been neither particularly engaging for me nor very relevant to my life outside the school system. Instead of acquiring the real-world skills they needed, my students were acquiring *school skills*: skills like cramming for an exam or determining how to ignore information that wouldn't be on a test—skills that help students progress in the school system but don't help when they leave it.

As I struggled with the realization that my teaching was ineffective, I began looking for an alternative to the traditional teaching approach I had unconsciously adopted. My goal was to devise an engaging instructional approach that wouldn't unduly add to my already demanding workload—an approach that would require my students to use higher-level thinking and result in their learning relevant skills that would equip them for success in the modern world. After much trial-and-error experimentation, I devised a method of instruction that met my goal. I call this method the *problems-first* approach to instruction. It allows students to learn higher-level thinking skills and essential, enduring process skills at the same time as they are learning the curriculum. This approach is based on giving students a problem without telling them the information they need to solve it. Giving the problem first before you do any teaching encourages students to take on a more active role in the learning process because it makes the students responsible for acquiring the information that is necessary for creating a successful solution. The *problems-first* approach goes hand in hand with a structured problem-solving process I have developed called the *four Ds*. The four Ds provide students with a process to follow that will equip them to tackle real-world problems.

I have been very pleased with the independence that has been fostered in students since I began using the problems-first approach along with the four Ds. What has been truly gratifying is the feedback I have received from students who have graduated and then reported back to me the success they have experienced in their chosen career due to their ability to solve problems independently.

This book is primarily intended for upper elementary, middle, and high school teachers facing the task of engaging students in content-laden courses while also trying to teach 21st century thinking skills to modern students of the digital generation. It may also be useful for postsecondary instructors. The teaching technique outlined in these pages can be applied in almost all subject areas to content that lends itself to a project-based approach. While teachers are encouraged to incorporate at least one problems-first project in each term, it is possible to teach entire courses using the problems-first approach.

This book is divided into three parts. Part one is devoted to understanding the needs of students in a digital generation and introducing a new approach to teaching—the *problems-first* approach. Chapter 1 discusses the inadequacies of the traditional lecture-style approach and the reasons why a new instructional approach is so desperately needed in education. Chapter 2 introduces readers to the skills students *do* need for long-term success in life after school—higher-level thinking and seven process skills to allow students to adapt to and solve problems that arise in any aspect of their lives. These skills are the foundation of the problems-first method. Chapter 3 articulates the key to this new approach—presenting the curriculum content in the form of a problem to solve.

In part two, readers discover how to create problems-first projects. This is the how-to part of the book, where you will find directions for how to implement the problems-first instructional approach. Chapters 4 through 12 each introduce a step for teachers to take in creating problems-first projects. In short, these steps include the following.

- Envision a new role for the teacher.
- Ensure that problems are first and teaching is second.
- Establish a real-world link using role-play.
- Equip students with the four Ds of problem solving.
- Expand your view of the curriculum.
- Elevate the students' level of thought.
- Educate the whole mind.
- Evaluate holistically.
- Ease yourself out of the picture.

Within the chapters in part two, readers encounter the *four Ds* strategy for effective problem solving: (1) *d*efine the problem, (2) *d*esign the solution, (3) *d*o the work, and (4) *d*ebrief the product created and the process followed.

Finally, part three provides guidance on how to make the shift to a problems-first approach. Chapter 13 answers any questions readers may have on how to begin using this new approach in classrooms, and chapter 14 provides a number of problems-first projects, including rubrics, to help teachers plan projects.

Throughout the book, each chapter ends with Questions for Discussion, which allows readers to consider each aspect of this new teaching method in depth either individually or as part of a teacher team.

Please note: This book discusses proficiency with technology as part of its discussion of essential process skills necessary for life. In the past when I have listed technological proficiency as a necessary part of learning three-dimensional thinking and the seven pillar process skills, many educators responded by telling me they couldn't teach these kinds of skills because their schools didn't have the necessary technology. But the thinking and skills mentioned in this book, which are more valuable than technological skills in and of themselves, can be taught with whatever tools you have available to you, even if you don't have the latest electronic technology. Of course, you should be using technology when you can, and you should be advocating to get the latest and most powerful technological tools into the hands of your students. But the use of technological tools is not absolutely essential for teaching students three-dimensional thinking and the seven pillar process skills they need for success in the future.

There are many strategies for teaching differently, and the problems-first method I propose in this book represents one more instructional arrow in a teacher's quiver of instructional approaches. It is my hope that teachers will comprehend the power of the problems-first instructional approach; that they will see that this approach encourages the development of valuable process skills that will empower their students to step out of school into lifelong success. While this approach to instruction that I propose may seem uncomfortable to employ at first, I have seen many teachers embrace the problems-first approach with very favorable results for their students.

PART ONE

Understanding New Needs and a New Approach for a Digital Generation

With the rise of the internet, mass communication, and instantaneous access to information, students in the 21st century need different skills for employment and life after graduation than students in the 20th. In the first part of this book, we will discuss the changing needs of students in our classrooms today, how that differs from what students' needs used to be, and how traditional teaching methods are inadequate for equipping our current students for success in any age, but particularly in this new digital world.

Chapter 1 discusses the inadequacies of the traditional lecture-style approach and the reasons why a new instructional approach is so desperately needed in education. Chapter 2 introduces readers to the skills students *do* need for long-term success in life after school—higher-level thinking and seven process skills to allow students to adapt to problems that arise in any aspect of their lives—and describes how these skills are the foundation of the problems-first teaching method. Chapter 3 lays out the key to this new approach—presenting the curriculum content in the form of a problem to solve.

CHAPTER 1

The New Needs of a Changing Generation

Teaching is a complex task. A teacher must, of course, have knowledge of the subject and content he or she teaches, but there is much more to effective instruction than knowledge of content. Teachers must also understand the developmental psychology of the students they are teaching and the skills necessary for success in the modern world. In addition, teachers must cultivate strategies with which to convey concepts and information to the individuals they teach. These strategies, and the techniques teachers use to devise them, change and improve with experience, but they can also change out of necessity and the need to adapt to the changing needs of a new generation of students.

Teaching differently does not mean that we should throw away everything we currently do. We need to assess the efficacy of what we do. We must keep what is valid and discard what isn't. However, we must incorporate into our teaching what current educational research has to offer and come to grips with a changing world and the changing nature of students in that world.

This chapter will discuss the current state of teaching in North America and assess one of the most pervasive methods of teaching—the *teaching as telling, learning as listening* method. It will consider the experience students have when teachers use this method and compare the resulting skills students acquire with those that the great educational theorists (from Dewey, Montessori, and Piaget to Bloom, Bruner, Papert, and Marzano) say they need in order to thrive in the modern workforce. Will the skills acquired through traditional teaching and the skills needed to thrive reflect one another, or will they be different? A knowledge of the current situation in schools and the problems that pervasive teaching methods can cause students prepares readers to shift their instructional mindsets to more effective methods for the digital age.

The Situation in Schools

A few years into my teaching career, I began looking for the rationale underlying why I taught the way I did because my instruction was not developing long-term independent learning skills in my students. I decided to canvass my colleagues, asking them to explain the rationale for their personal instructional approaches. I thought I might gain insight into my methods as a teacher by learning how they thought about and articulated their own methods. I immediately ran into a major problem. Many of my colleagues hadn't really considered the underlying rationale for their method of instruction; they, like I had for so long, just taught the same way they had been taught as students. As a result, the way my fellow teachers and I were teaching was simply a product of repetition rather than a deliberate effort to teach in a manner that would be most beneficial to student learning.

There is an invisible force that shapes the approach we educators take to teaching young people. This force is our mindset—our way of thinking. My colleagues and I taught based on an established mindset, but without being aware of what that mindset was. Like everyone who passes through the school system, we absorbed the mindset for this kind of teaching, almost by osmosis, as it was modeled by our own teachers when we were students. It is critical that we understand there is a way of thinking about instruction that has been in place for so long that many educators accept it without really considering why. Parents, students, teachers, administrators, and politicians have all accepted this mindset for instruction without question. It is so pervasive and established that we often simply assume that this is the only way to teach, without considering the rationale behind it or its effect on students in an increasingly technological world. Even younger teachers who have grown up in the digital world are not free from the effects of the established mindset for instruction because they have been subjected to teaching based on this mindset by their older teachers.

The current mindset that was entrenched in our school system early in the 1900s, and that often shapes teaching even in 2020, is based on an early 20th century rationale inspired by Henry Ford's assembly-line model for manufacturing. According to Linda Darling-Hammond (1997) in *The Right to Learn*, in 1908, William Wirt came up with the idea of the *platoon school*, in which students would move through the school just like cars moved on the assembly line. Darling-Hammond (1997) states:

> Hoping to save on wasted plant space and solve overcrowding in schools, Wirt devised a system in which students circulate through the school from one classroom to another, with different teachers teaching them different subjects for short periods of time. (p. 41)

The idea was to reap efficiency benefits from applying a mass instruction approach to education. The emphasis shifted from addressing the learning needs of individual students to disseminating information to groups of students through a lecture style of instruction. The phrase *teaching as telling, learning as listening* captures the essence of this long-standing, traditional mindset for instruction. In this method, learning consists mainly of students listening while the teacher tells them what they need to know about a subject. The teacher is the center of attention while he or she lectures and is the only one in the classroom who is supposed to be active while he or she gives the lesson. Students sit passively and listen as the teacher talks. The teacher is focused on content delivery by telling the students what he or she knows about this topic. An important factor in the assessment of learning in this approach is memorization. Teachers view students as vessels to be filled with information and procedures. Students demonstrate their learning by their ability to recall the material presented by the teacher. Students take notes as the teacher talks as the first step in memorizing details in preparation for a written test. Teaching comes first in this approach, followed by reading and project work to reinforce the instruction. The teacher must devote a significant amount of time to managing student behavior because this kind of instruction is often not very engaging. Figure 1.1 (page 10) offers an example of what a teaching as telling, learning as listening lesson might look like in a junior high social studies classroom. Although this lesson is a hypothetical, it's likely that educators and students alike will recognize many features within this lesson from their own classroom experiences.

It continually amazes me how universal this kind of teaching is. Everyone I talk to has experienced this kind of instruction, in which the teacher talks and the students listen. This is instruction that focuses on content delivery. Instruction that rewards those who can remember the details in the material that has been presented. Instruction that focuses on summative evaluation in the form of a written test. Instruction that uses the written test as a major motivation for memorizing the information in the lesson.

This lecture approach to teaching and learning is so pervasive in schools today it is impossible to escape its influence. It shapes the way virtually everything is done in our schools, especially in high schools and postsecondary institutions. This continues to be the case even though we know that the lecture style of instruction is one of the least effective ways to teach (Daub, 2014; Strauss, 2017). It doesn't matter where you live, whether you are a teacher who grew up in the 1960s or 1970s before microcomputer technology exploded into life or one who grew up using computer technology in the 1980s or 1990s or even a teacher who grew up in the internet era of the new millennium. Everyone who attended a typical high school has been bombarded with the teaching as telling, learning as listening approach to instruction. There are some variations in teaching strategy, of course, but the underlying approach remains the same.

I have observed that some teachers are resistant to moving away from long-standing, familiar notions of how to teach. I believe that this is largely due to the pervasiveness of the mindset that informs teaching as telling, learning as listening, along with humankind's natural aversion to change. Other teachers may be aware that teaching as telling, learning as listening is not as effective as they had hoped, but they may not have the knowledge or confidence to move away from familiar strategies. Consequently, the mindset for instruction and its associated teaching strategies are not evolving as they should to best meet the changing needs of students in the modern world.

> The teacher begins the class by saying, "All right, the bell has gone. Please stop talking and get out your notebooks. We have been talking about the Allied invasion of Europe from Great Britain during World War II. As I mentioned, the invasion took place on June 6, 1944. Last class we covered the landings by American troops on the Utah and Omaha beaches, and I'll give you your test scores on that material later in this period. Today, we are going to look at the landings in the British sector.
>
> "We will start with Juno Beach. This beach lies to the east of where the American soldiers landed. The attack on this beach fell to the Canadian 3rd Infantry Division."
>
> The teacher looks up from his lesson notes and sees a student with his notebook closed and his head propped up on his hands.
>
> "Bobby, your notebook isn't even open! Why aren't you taking notes?"
>
> "I don't have a pen," Bobby replies sheepishly.
>
> "Well, borrow one!" says the teacher.
>
> Bobby turns around to ask the girl sitting behind him for a pen, and she hands him one. Bobby turns back toward the teacher, holds the pen out over his notebook, and plunks his head down on his other hand
>
> "Okay. Now, where was I?" asks the teacher. "Oh yes. The Canadian landing craft faced a difficult situation. The beach obstacles were partially submerged, and the engineers were unable to clear paths to the beach. The landing craft were forced to avoid the obstacles, and mines took a heavy toll on the boats. Roughly thirty percent of the landing craft at Juno were destroyed before they reached the beach. As the troops waded ashore, there was little fire at first because the German gun positions did not aim out to sea. Instead, they were set to enfilade the coastline. As the Canadian soldiers worked their way up the beach and came into the enfilading killing zones, they took dreadful casualties."
>
> "What does 'enfilade the coastline' mean?" asks a girl in the class.
>
> "It's where the guns create an inverted V-shaped trap where the further in you go, the more crossfire you get," replies the teacher. "After heavy fighting, troops managed to get off the beach. Armored units arrived later in the day, and one unit briefly cut off the Caen-Bayeux Road. This one Canadian tank regiment was the only unit of the entire Allied invasion to reach its final objective on D-Day."
>
> The teacher again looks up from his notes and sees two students talking.
>
> "Natalie and Jim, please stop talking and pay attention."
>
> The teacher then hands out a written assignment to the students.
>
> "Now, I want you to write a report on the Canadian landings using the section on Juno Beach in chapter five in your textbooks. The report must include a map of the beaches and list all the objectives for the Canadians. There will be bonus marks if the map is colored. The report needs to be at least three pages long if you want an 'A' for your mark. And you all need to review your notes before next class because on Friday there's going to be a . . . "
>
> "Test," say all the students collectively.

Sources: *Copp, 2019; Drez, n.d.; "Juno Beach," n.d.*

Figure 1.1: Example of a teaching as telling, learning as listening lesson.

The Problems for Students

There are several major concerns with continuing to teach students with the teaching as telling, learning as listening approach.

First, memorization is a major focus of the teaching as telling, learning as listening approach, but the development of memorization skill is rarely an effective long-term learning mechanism. Think about when you were in school. These many years later, do you remember all the specific details from the classes you took? How well would you perform on a high school history or algebra test if you had to take the test today? Unless you teach these subjects, you would likely fail because you would have forgotten most of the details that were covered in those courses. When it comes to the information that we memorize, we are very much faced with a use-it-or-lose-it situation. Hermann Ebbinghaus described the loss of learned information in what has been called the *forgetting curve* (Wittman, n.d.). According to Ebbinghaus, without actively using or reviewing new information, we generally lose about 60 percent of what we have learned within twenty minutes of processing new material and 75 percent of what we have learned within two days (Wittman, n.d.). While it is worthwhile to note that memorization will always be a necessary component of learning—in order to think or speak intelligently about a topic, you must have in your mind at least some of the details on that subject—it is clear that students require much more than memorization of facts to produce meaningful learning that lasts.

In fact, the teaching as telling, learning as listening approach reflects little of what educational research over the last one hundred and fifty years has discovered about thinking and learning. If you follow the development of educational thought since the late 1800s, including great educational thinkers of modern times such as Maria Montessori (1912), Jean Piaget (1970), John Dewey (1990), Lev S. Vygotsky (1978), Abraham Maslow (1954), Benjamin S. Bloom (1956), Edgar Dale (1984), and William Glasser (1998), you will see a definite trend away from seeing teaching as telling and toward seeing teaching as facilitating higher-level thinking through active student participation in learning activities. Figure 1.2 (page 12), adapted from a figure I created with Nicky Mohan, shows a diagram of the progression from the lowest to the highest levels of learning that incorporates some of these major ideas.

This diagram illustrates the level of learning that results from various kinds of teaching strategies. It is important to see that teaching as telling, learning as listening falls into the lowest category, where students just listen to a teacher talk. One of the major reasons for the ineffectiveness of this instructional approach is that students do not play an active role in the learning. Teaching by telling treats students as containers and envisions learning predominantly as memorizing. The teacher's role becomes that of filling up students' minds with facts and procedures. Many teachers argue that they have updated their teaching to include photos, recordings, colorful websites, movies, and YouTube videos to enhance the learning in their classrooms. While this is laudable, it must be noted that including

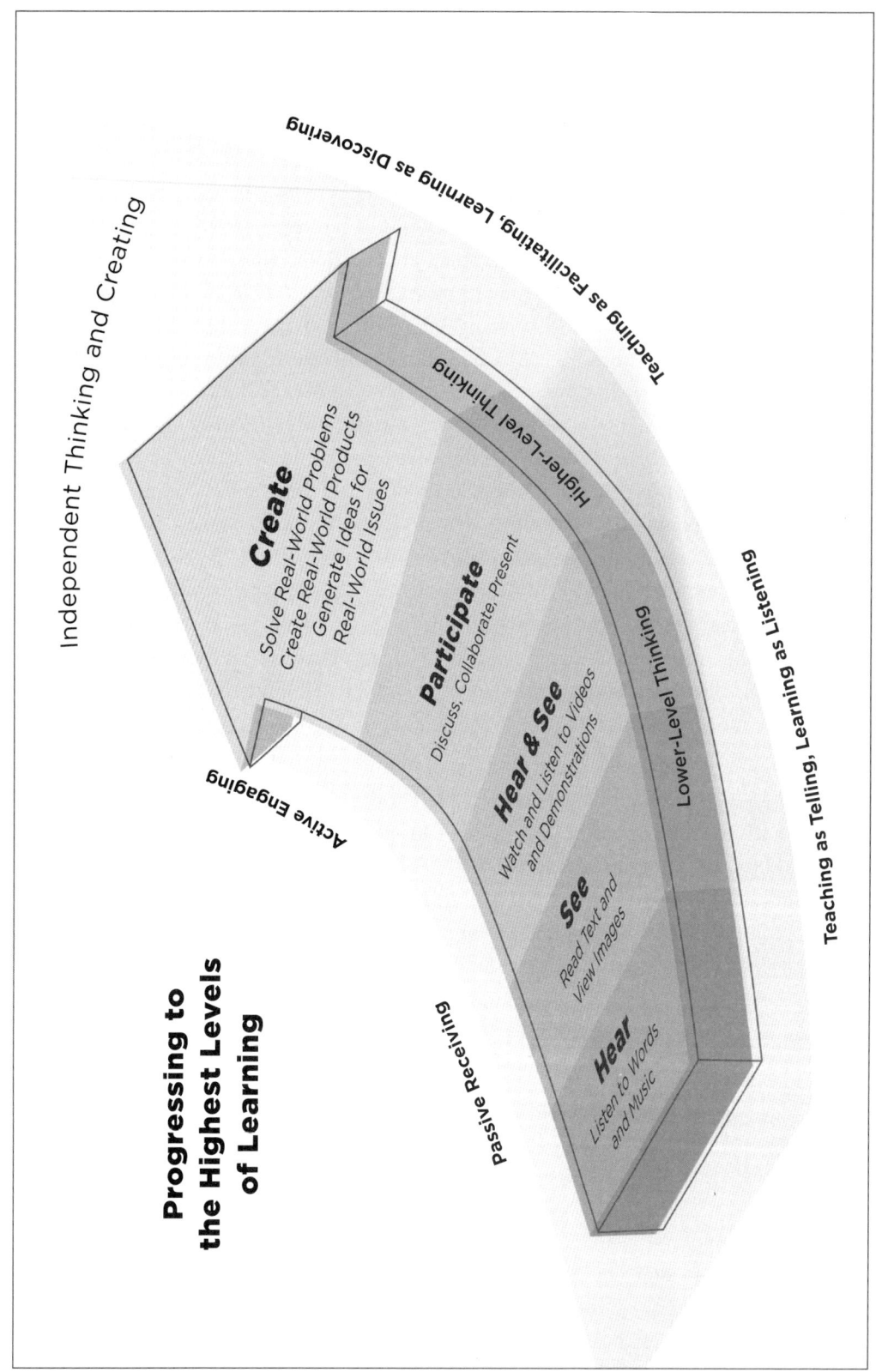

Figure 1.2: A visual summary of the ideas of great educational theorists.

multimedia presentations in instruction only progresses as far as the third category in the diagram, "Hear & See." Students still play a passive role in the learning process.

Additionally, the teaching as telling, learning as listening approach does not work well with modern students who have grown up in a digital world filled with networked technology. These students often have a radically different life experience than the adults who are teaching them. They live as much in the digital world as they do in the real world (Sulla, 2012). Many of these young people have already logged a great deal of time in the digital world before they ever set foot in a traditional school. They have grown up with highly interactive online digital experiences, complete with hyperlinks and multimedia. Their experience in this digital world caters to their individuality. They control the direction they want to go in this digital world, as well as the pace at which they travel. The services and games they use in the digital world offer them a wide range of personal choice and allow them to customize their experience to match their individual preferences. Ian Jukes, Lee Crockett, and I took an in-depth look at the attributes of young people today and the difficulties they have with the traditional school system. We outlined our findings in our book *Understanding the Digital Generation* (Jukes, McCain, & Crockett, 2010). Students of the digital generation have great difficulty learning when they encounter teaching as telling, learning as listening teachers who expect them to sit passively and listen when they are so used to interacting with the digital content.

One feature of contemporary life that particularly confronts the digital generation is the availability of information and content, and the subsequent effects on the skills modern students need for success in life both during and after school. In the 20th century, it was valuable to memorize content because seeking out an answer often took considerable time—students would have to look up logarithmic values in elaborate tables or visit libraries and trawl through many books to find information or answers to simple questions. In the 21st century, however, an astounding amount of content is available in mere seconds. The global reach of the internet, combined with the power of search tools like Google and the prevalence of personal digital devices such as smartphones or laptops, makes an enormous volume of information instantly available to anyone. Further, the increasing rate of change in the world today means that much of the information we encounter has a short shelf life before it is superseded by more up-to-date information (Butler, 2016). Consequently, it is often better to access information at the time that you need it. Thus, the problems many students face with information in the digital age relate not to *accessing* content—that much is simple—but rather to *parsing* it and *thinking* about it. In the age of information overload, memorization is no longer the priority. The skills students need to succeed, both in middle and secondary school as well as in the workforce, are now *processing skills*. For example, how do students identify the correct information when a Google search returns over 1,000,000 results? How should they make sense of sources that may conflict each other? Where is the best place to go to begin gathering information to solve a problem? These are all skills students can transfer to the modern workplace to bring value to a company. The needs of students have changed dramatically in the 21st century, and our teaching methods must therefore adapt accordingly.

Conclusion

Although the traditional teaching as telling, learning as listening method of instruction is pervasive, it is not the most effective strategy for either student learning itself or preparation for the workforce and life after school. While memorization and recollection may have been important skills in the 20th century, the rise of the internet and the sheer accessibility of information in the millennial world greatly diminishes the importance of those skills. A new instructional method is needed to better prepare students for the digitally driven world they live in.

The task of finding a new approach to teaching is a formidable one. This new teaching strategy must incorporate the ideas of great educational thinkers, and it must be an approach that will work effectively for the students of today as well as those of tomorrow. Most importantly, this strategy must inspire educators with the idea of teaching differently and give them confidence that this method will help students succeed. We educators cannot continue to teach the same way that we have in the past and expect that our instruction will produce different results.

Before discussing a new instructional method, we must first consider the skills students *do* need for success in the digital age. The next chapter will focus on these skills and why they are essential for student learning.

QUESTIONS FOR DISCUSSION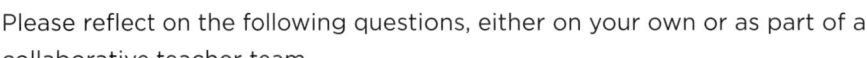

Please reflect on the following questions, either on your own or as part of a collaborative teacher team.

1. Consider what your own learning experience was like when you were a high school student. What kind of teaching did you experience? Did you mostly sit and listen as your teachers talked? How applicable was the content to your life after school? How engaged were you?

2. Assess your current teaching practice. Do you talk or lecture most of the time, or do you encourage students to take charge of their learning? Do students ask questions frequently during your lessons? Do your assessments focus mostly on content recall? Is the content you teach driven mostly by what will be on state, provincial, or national standardized tests? How much did your student experience influence your ideas for how to teach?

3. Think about your goals for your teaching in the future. If you could make any change to your teaching method, what would it be? Considering the global economy and the implications it has for the nature of work in the 21st century, what skills do you wish you could impart to your students?

CHAPTER 2

The Thinking and Processing Skills Students Need for the Future

The skills students are currently learning in school through the teaching as telling, learning as listening model differ vastly from the skills employers are seeking in new hires. *The Future of Jobs* report, published by the World Economic Forum (2016), features a list of the top ten skills that people will need for success in the world of work in 2020. These skills are:

1. Complex problem solving
2. Critical thinking
3. Creativity
4. People management
5. Coordinating with others
6. Emotional intelligence
7. Judgement and decision making
8. Service orientation
9. Negotiation
10. Cognitive flexibility

None of these skills feature the memorizing of facts and procedures that is the focus of the teaching as telling, learning as listening approach. For a lot of teaching, memorization has traditionally been the ceiling. However, the needs of the contemporary workforce require educators to see memorization not as the ceiling, but rather as the floor—the foundation for more significant cognitive work students must do.

Thinking of memorization as the floor rather than the ceiling represents an incredibly important shift in thinking for teachers. It is key to facilitating active learning that *lasts*. Memorization skills predominantly focus on preparing students for taking tests. Once the test has been completed, students often no longer need to remember the content they have learned. However, long-term learning often occurs when students are taught *process skills*—thinking skills used when doing something. Examples include reading, writing, problem solving, and information processing.

Process skills are transferable skills. Teaching someone a process skill enables them to apply that skill in a wide variety of situations that have yet to be encountered because, even if the specific details are different, the methods they have learned can still be applied to the new task. This is the power of process learning. Process skills endure. They never expire. These skills, requiring higher-level thinking than rote repetition from memory, engender long-term learning that will endure well after teaching is done and students have forgotten specific content.

When students enter the school system, we start out on the right track, equipping our young students with useful processes such as reading, writing, and arithmetic skills which they can use again and again in a variety of situations. We don't just teach students how to write only one paragraph; we teach them the writing process so they can compose letters, reports, essays, stories, and more. We don't just teach young students how to add only one sample of numbers; we teach them the process of addition so they can do a variety of calculations. When teaching them how to read, we don't just teach them how to read one story. Instead, we teach them the process of reading so they are equipped to read a variety of written materials. We should continue this strategy by teaching our middle and high school students process skills that will equip them to process information to perform tasks, solve problems, and form fact-based opinions both in the school environment and in life after graduation.

Process learning is ideally suited to *project-based learning* (PBL). The project-based learning approach to teaching fosters students' acquisition of knowledge and skills by having them work for an extended period of time to investigate and respond to an authentic, engaging, and complex question, problem, or challenge (Buck Institute for Education, n.d.; Wolpert-Gawron, 2015). The goals of PBL are threefold: (1) to have students learn course content through discovery learning, (2) to develop the long-term process skills necessary to solve real-world problems, and as a result, (3) to foster independence in students. Process skills like problem solving, critical thinking, and information investigation are needed for students to independently tackle PBL projects.

Learning through projects also provides a relevant context that facilitates learning the details of course content and important process skills. Context is essential for helping students remember information and, thus, perform well on the written exams they will undoubtedly face (Osth, 2019). Not only does PBL encourage process skill development, it also can have a very positive impact on student achievement (Duke & Halvorsen, 2017; Kingston, 2018).

Thus, a more effective instructional approach for preparing students for life after graduation should be project based and must focus on higher-level thinking and process skills. But what are those process skills? This chapter will first discuss the precursor to process skills—three-dimensional thinking—and show how this sort of thinking is not only more beneficial than the more one-dimensional thinking memorization requires, but also advantageous in the workforce. It will then introduce the seven pillars of success—seven process skills, highly desired in the modern workplace, that extend students' perspectives and, in combination, exercise all three dimensions of thinking. These skills are what educators must focus on if they wish to prepare students for success in life after graduation.

The Key to Thinking in the Future— Three-Dimensional Thinking

The skills needed for success in the world of work in 2020, listed at the beginning of this chapter, are all process skills. This is a much different list of skills than what was needed in the past (Hathaway, n.d.; Quast, 2011), and developing these skills will require students to use more robust thinking than what was previously required for success in the world outside school (Gray, 2017). I call this more robust thinking *three-dimensional thinking* because it is thought that involves the three major aspects of the full spectrum of a person's cognition—convergent thinking, divergent thinking, and metacognitive thinking (Rothstein & Santana, 2011). *Convergent thinking* is the ability to think logically. It involves synthesizing an array of ideas and facts to make sense of it all. This is the intellectual activity that allows students to summarize, explain, interpret, compare, and contrast by pulling various concepts and details together from the information they have discovered. *Divergent thinking* is the ability to generate a broad range of ideas, options, hypotheses, and possibilities. Instead of a focus on getting the right answer, divergent thinking is concerned more with the process of *how* one arrives at an answer, recognizing that there may be different ways to get there. *Metacognition* is the ability to focus inward and assess one's own learning and thinking processes and habits of mind. Metacognition is what enables us to identify what we are good at, what we need to work on, and what steps we need to take to address the areas of our thinking and learning that need improvement (Rothstein & Santana, 2011). These different elements of thinking are illustrated in figure 2.1 on page 18.

Three-dimensional thinking skills represent the full range of cognitive skill that people will need for success in the future; however, most students do not complete high school with the divergent thinking skills necessary for effective problem solving,

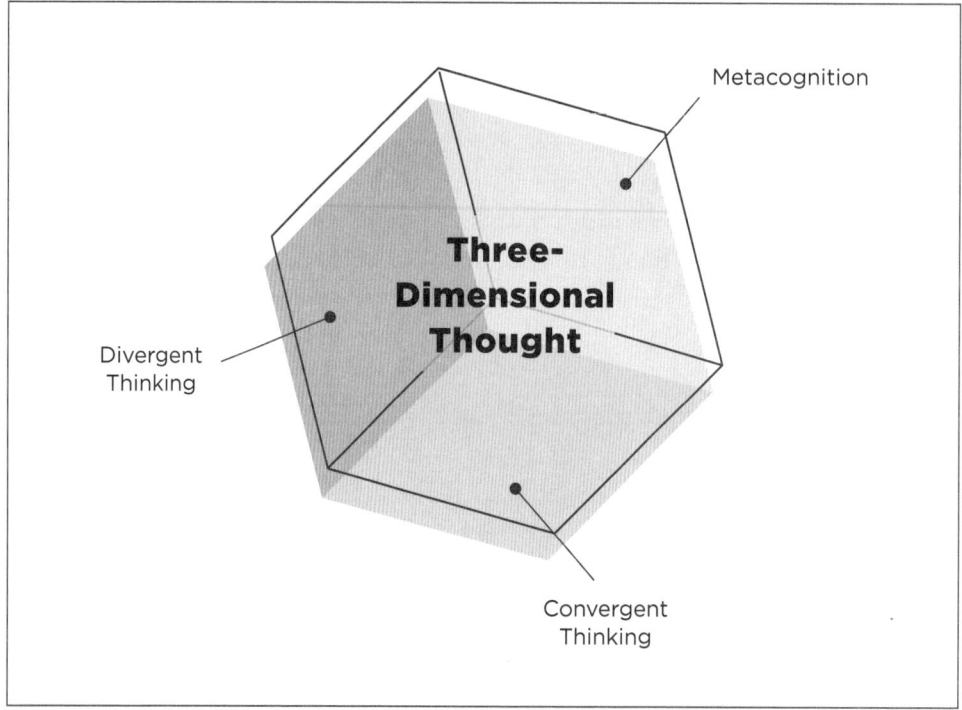

Figure 2.1: The three major aspects of thinking.

innovation, and creativity, and the metacognitive thinking skills necessary for objective self-evaluation. That's because schools tend to have a narrow definition of intelligence centered on convergent thought (Luenendonk, 2019). Teaching emphasizes and rewards the application of logical deductive thought, analytical skills, and rational reasoning in courses like mathematics, science, geography, history, business, and shop (building and design) classes. And although these courses offer many opportunities for divergent and metacognitive thinking, the rise of standardized testing over the last thirty years has significantly narrowed the focus of instruction and assessment on convergent thought. Even courses like English and English literature have been impacted by the push for standardized assessment. In addition, in classes where brainstorming, journaling, and mind mapping do occur, it has been my observation that assessment in those classes does not adequately evaluate the development of divergent and metacognitive thinking. It is a common experience for a teacher to be leading students in a lively discussion of creative ideas that spring from some aspect of course content only to have the discussion come to a complete stop when a student asks, "Is this going to be on the test?" We must broaden our teaching and assessment to include the full range of three-dimensional thinking because all three aspects of it are critical components of the kind of effective, innovative thought that is increasingly needed for success in the modern world.

The Seven Pillars of Success

I have identified seven essential process skills that require students to use the entire spectrum of three-dimensional thinking skills so that they will be empowered for personal and professional achievement for the rest of their lives. These *seven pillars of success* are the skills that allow practical application of three-dimensional thinking (see figure 2.2). These seven skills are:

1. Internal attitude skills
2. Information investigation skills
3. Imagination creativity skills
4. Innovation creativity skills
5. Interpersonal skills
6. Interdependent collaboration skills
7. Independent problem-solving skills

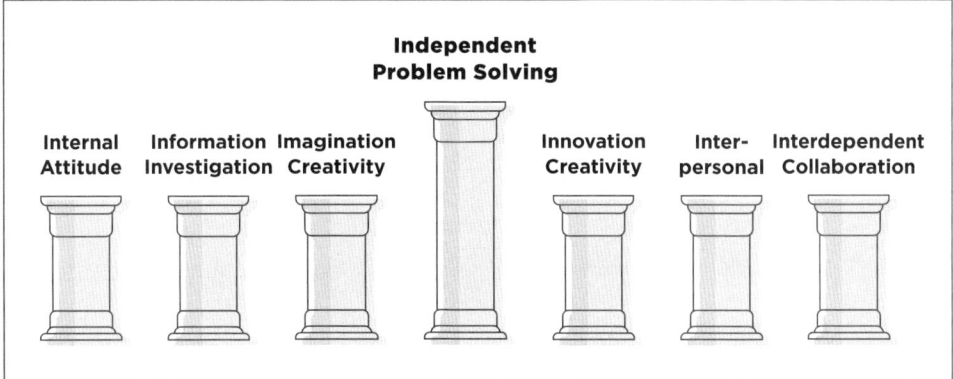

Figure 2.2: The seven pillars of success—process skills every student needs.

Pillar 1: Internal Attitude Skills

Ask any teacher, and he or she will tell you that a student's attitude toward work is of the utmost importance to the student's success. Attitude enables students to gain personal awareness and develop intentional strategies to achieve positive personal outcomes, and this is why internal attitude skills are so important.

I break internal attitude skills into two categories: (1) personal attitude skills and (2) productive attitude skills. Personal attitude skills include honesty, self-confidence, patience, open-mindedness, the ability to manage one's emotions, the ability to be truthful with oneself by objectively assessing one's own strengths and weaknesses, and the choice to be a positive person regardless of the circumstances. Productive attitude skills are what one needs to be a productive person. These include a willingness and determination to learn, time management, self-motivation, the ability to take initiative, the ability to overcome boredom, perseverance when things are difficult, self-evaluation of one's own work, and long-term goal setting. Developing these attitudes will make students more productive not only in their schoolwork but in whatever career they pursue when they leave the school system.

Learning to think critically about one's habits of mind is an important part of developing metacognitive skills. In an age when employers contract out more and more work to individual entrepreneurs, the metacognitive skill of introspection is essential not only for personal growth but also to ensure that the quality of one's work is continually improving and relevant in a competitive marketplace.

Teaching goals need to make acquiring internal attitude skills explicit, and teachers should assess students' progress in developing them. Teachers cannot evaluate these skills with a written test, so they must broaden their assessment strategies to include the use of rubrics. Rubrics enable a teacher to focus on a particular attitude skill and assess a student's development of that skill. For example, when assessing a student's positive attitude, a rubric provides the tool to assess whether a student is never positive, is positive some of the time, is positive most of the time, or is positive all of the time. (See chapter 11, page 99, for a more complete discussion of rubrics.)

Student self-assessment is the most valuable tool for evaluating internal attitude skills because only students really know what is going on with their attitudes. Self-assessment involves metacognitive thinking, and it is possibly the best tool for developing this kind of thought. Research by John Hattie and Shirley Clarke (2019) shows that self-assessment by students has a significant positive effect on learning while freeing up the teacher from the burden of evaluating all work done in the classroom. In addition, once students leave the school system, self-assessment becomes a valuable personal tool that will empower individuals to achieve success in the workplace (Saba, n.d.).

Pillar 2: Information Investigation Skills

Dealing with a limitless volume of data in all its forms, both written and visual, is not the only challenge students will face in the modern world. As I have discussed, of greater concern is determining the quality and reliability of that information. People need to have the ability to evaluate the information they discover. We as teachers need to equip our students with information investigation skills so they can investigate a specific topic, find data that are pertinent to their investigation, assess the reliability of the information that they have retrieved, and, finally, determine its meaning. Having the ability to evaluate information to determine its reliability, value, and relevancy gives a person great power in the new information landscape (Kirton & Barham, 2005). We need to equip our students with high-level cognitive skills so they can process the data they encounter and turn it into meaningful information that is useful for the task at hand. Teaching students to critically assess the information they acquire is an excellent way to equip them with convergent thinking skills.

To develop this skill, educators can teach their students to use the *Ask-Probe-Evaluate* structured process when investigating information (see table 2.1).

Table 2.1: The Ask-Probe-Evaluate Process

Step	Definition	Example
Ask	Ask questions to identify, define, and pinpoint the task that is the reason for researching new information.	Why is this task being done? What are the specifics of the task to be done? What information is needed to complete this task? Who has that information? Where is that information located?
Probe	Explore a range of sources for information and acquire the raw data. For online investigation, apply the Boolean search techniques (using "and," "or," or "not" logic) required by online search engines to find the information you are looking for.	Use online search engines like Google, Bing, Yahoo, Yandex, Ask.com, and DuckDuckGo. Also explore books, magazines, journals, and interviews with people who have relevant knowledge.
Evaluate	Analyze the retrieved data; determine its validity and relevance to the task at hand; perform calculations, draw conclusions, and form opinions based on the data.	Check the background of the author, assess the subjectivity of the author, assess how believable the information is, determine if there is support from others that affirms this information, ask what can be learned about this information by calculating statistics from it. (See chapter 9, page 77, for a more complete discussion of information analysis.)

We want students to comprehend what they find, not just regurgitate it. We want students to demonstrate understanding, not just robotically echo what they have been told. We want them to apply what they have learned, not just acquire theoretical knowledge.

Pillar 3: Imagination Creativity Skills

Imagination creativity skills are all about using one's imagination to conceive an original idea to create something new. Imagination is an aspect of divergent thinking that empowers a person to add meaning, value, and beauty to a project.

An important application of creativity is the use of imagination to communicate information beyond using words. Communicating using just text has been superseded in the contemporary world by the audiovisual presentation of information. Graphic design is now an important—even critical—aspect of printed material, websites, and videos (Wowbix Marketing, 2019). Let me be clear: words are no longer enough. I am not saying that we shouldn't teach the writing process to our students, but I am saying that because the vehicle of presentation for the majority of daily communication no longer consists of just words, we must also teach our students modern audiovisual communication skills, and the flexibility of mind to choose from among multiple communication mediums—putting to use flexible thinking is an important part of being creative. Modern information communication skills include an understanding of:

- Graphic design
- Typography
- Color
- Photo composition
- Video composition
- Sound production

Students should be encouraged to learn these aspects of modern audiovisual communication and apply them to their project work in all courses.

Another aspect of imagination creativity is using one's imagination to create a design that will add value to something beyond its function. For example, Apple adds value to their products through distinctive exterior shape. Apple's goal is to make their products more desirable than those of their competitors through their imaginative design.

Imagination creativity goes beyond adding value to functional things. Imagination can be used to create an item whose value is derived purely from its beauty. The product doesn't have to serve a function. Its value comes from its shape, color, texture, or sound. These aesthetic elements provide some of the reasons for why people buy a sculpture or work of art or a piece of music.

Educators can teach imagination creativity skills just like any other skill. In the book *The Myth of the Muse*, Douglas Reeves and Brooks Reeves (2017) argue that creativity is not just something that is spontaneous or that a person is born with, but rather that it is a process that can be cultivated by utilizing seven virtues that inspire creativity:

curiosity, versatility, synthesis, discipline, collaboration, experimentation, and tenacity. Teachers can give projects to students that are structured to require imagination in order to complete the task. An example would be having students write a noun and a verb on two pieces of paper and then put their words in two different jars labelled "Noun" and "Verb." Students would draw one noun and verb randomly from each jar and then draw a picture showing the relationship between the two words. Another example would be to ask students to write a fact-based fictional conversation between Martin Luther King Jr. and the current president on the topic of the status of civil rights in the United States.

Imagination creativity skills are not taught in the majority of courses in the school system today, especially not in higher grades. Unless students take courses in art, drama, music, or creative writing, they are likely to graduate from school without significantly developing their imagination creativity skills. This must change if we hope to prepare our students for the world of the future.

Pillar 4: Innovation Creativity Skills

The government, the school system, and the economy all run on *ideas*. Businesses are constantly looking for new ideas to gain competitive advantage, the field of medicine is always looking for new ideas for treatments and cures—simply put, ideas make the world go round. There is a universal need for ideas that will improve something that already exists as well as bring entirely new ideas to reality (Planbox, 2019). Regardless of the field, employers will always seek out people with the ability to generate new and improved ideas. There is a great need for people who are creators and innovators. This is especially true in our technological world because generating ideas is a uniquely human skill, unable to be automated.

There is a major misconception that the ability to innovate is genetic—that some people have the ability while some don't. Certainly, some people are better at innovating than others, but all of us have the capacity to come up with new ideas. Everyone is capable of innovation creativity (Henley, 2015; Reeves & Reeves, 2017).

There are two aspects to innovation creativity. First, creative thinking can be used to improve something that already exists (for example, changing the design of an airport terminal to improve the flow of people through the building). Second, innovative thinking is needed to invent something entirely new, such as developing an entirely new zero-emission method for powering a vehicle that does not require gasoline or electricity.

There is a great need for teachers to create an environment in their classrooms that fosters innovative thought—an environment where students can generate new ideas freely without worrying about getting it right or fearing what will happen if they are wrong. It is critical we remember that failure is at the very center of learning. Many of the great advances in our society have come from people like Thomas Edison who struggled mightily while inventing the light bulb—people who have been willing to try and fail repeatedly on their way to achieving success (Hendry, 2013).

So, if trying new things and failing at them is a central part of learning and necessary to be successful, then educators need to provide a learning environment where they encourage trying—even if that includes possibly failing. Instead, following the ubiquitous emphasis on high-pressure tests that students get only one chance to take, the focus is on the grade, not on learning and improvement (Miller, 2015). Almost every party involved views failure on these tests, which are often mandated at the federal level, as a negative thing, and so, unintentionally, educators create an environment that is counterproductive to innovative thinking. Instead, those who succeed in school are those who follow the rules and do as they are told (Barker, 2017). Divergent thinking is not generally appreciated or rewarded. But unlike school, life does not have strict rules, and the conformity that is rewarded in school does not lead to the kind of innovative thinking that is needed in the world today.

If students are to more fully develop the process skill of innovation creativity, we must find ways to create a positive learning environment in which they have the freedom to try out new ideas without the fear of failure. Brainstorming is an excellent way to make this happen because withholding criticism is one of the key principles of this process (McConnell, 2019). I will discuss how to incorporate idea generation into your classroom more fully in chapter 10 (page 89).

Pillar 5: Interpersonal Skills

With the rapid emergence of new communication platforms into our daily lives such as email, texting, Twitter, Facebook, Snapchat, Instagram, and many others, you would think that online communication skills using digital tools would be the most important set of personal communication skills students need to acquire in the technology-driven contemporary world. Developing these digital online communication skills is very valuable, but face-to-face communication skills—also known as *interpersonal skills*—remain the most important communication skills people need for success in the world today. Interpersonal communication skills—which include such things as the ability to conduct a conversation; listen with comprehension; understand nonverbal communication; persuade, debate, convince, sell, or defend a position; ask questions; communicate respectfully; accept criticism and give criticism constructively; and assert oneself—are all skills that are essential to functioning effectively in a family, in friendships, and in the workplace. From a workforce perspective, many companies are specifically looking for these skills when they interview potential employees because they are vital for working in teams, dealing with clients, and effective marketing (Phillpott, 2019).

Interestingly, technology is making interpersonal communication skills more essential than ever. The rapid growth in the power of smart machines and autonomous robots threatens to replace a great many jobs that humans have traditionally done. It is projected that by 2025 smart machines will perform more work than human workers, greatly changing the nature of work (Chowdhry, 2018). To ensure that future generations are not casualties in the rise of smart technology, they must develop skills that cannot easily be replaced by smart machines. Face-to-face human communication is one of those skill areas that remains solely in the domain of humans, and, thus, its importance will grow as smart technology makes some traditional jobs obsolete and allows other, more communication-based jobs to arise. Jobs that require "human skills," like sales and marketing, innovation, and customer service, are projected to increase dramatically in the near future (Chowdhry, 2018). This will happen, in part, because as machines take over many of the day-to-day operations of a business, employees with interpersonal skills will be needed to handle customer service. In banking, for example, smart machines already receive check deposits and handle withdrawal slips. It is increasingly important for bank tellers to demonstrate interpersonal skills such as friendliness and the ability to calm disgruntled customers (King, 2018).

Of course, students will use some interpersonal communication skills every day in every course, but a broader spectrum of these skills must become explicit teaching goals. The importance of these skills to our students' futures means we can't just expect students to develop them on their own.

Pillar 6: Interdependent Collaboration Skills

According to MyHub, if you look at any job description, there will be some requirement for the job holder to work as part of a team (Team MyHub, 2020). In fact, teamwork and collaboration are becoming such a vital part of the modern workplace that employers are now starting to use group tests to gauge how well prospective employees interact with one another (Randstad, n.d.). It is clear that collaboration skills have become an essential in the world of work.

There are many reasons for this, the first being the increased specialization in the world today. Take the design of a Boeing 787, for example. A Boeing 787 has dozens of specialists working on the engines alone. Then there are the controls, the hydraulics, and the airframe itself. Collaboration between those specialists is the only way to successfully make the airplane fly. It is the same for other projects at other manufacturers and other businesses (Stone, 2017). Another reason for the increase in the importance of collaboration is the change in the decision-making process in businesses today. No longer are all decisions made at the top, then dictated to workers from senior management. Many decisions in modern businesses are made collaboratively by those workers who have firsthand knowledge of the issues involved in the decision to be made (Blenko, Mankins, & Rogers, 2010; Filev, 2019).

The ability to collaborate on a project has always been an important skill because by working together, a group of people can be more productive than an individual alone can be. Interdependent collaboration skills include such things as the ability to criticize ideas without criticizing individuals, negotiate within a team, participate in group brainstorming and group problem solving, elicit and listen to feedback, take responsibility for designated tasks, and organize functional teams with members who complement one another.

The need for collaboration skills has increased considerably in the hyper-connected modern world. Global online communication and shared productivity tools like Skype, GoToMeeting, Zoom, and Google Docs are adding a new dimension to modern collaboration, as participants must work collaboratively with people who aren't physically in the same location. The ability to organize one's work and communicate clearly are especially important skills when working in a virtual group. Learning the skills to function effectively in virtual work groups has already become an essential skill for the modern world. This will only increase in the future. We need to provide opportunities for our students to work collaboratively in virtual groups as well as in face-to-face groups in the classroom.

Pillar 7: Independent Problem-Solving Skills

It is critical that students head into any career equipped with skills that employers cannot easily automate or outsource. One of the vital skill sets that students need to be employable both today and in the future is the ability to solve real-world, real-time problems. Daily life in the workplace is filled with problems; plus, as the technological world becomes more complex, the problems that people face in their normal working day become more complex as well. High-level independent problem solving used to be a task that only people in management performed. However, this is changing rapidly in the modern workplace. With technological tools becoming more powerful and ubiquitous, more and more frontline workers are involved in making decisions to help solve the problems that occur on a daily basis. Technology is providing these workers with the tools and the raw information they need to solve many of the issues they encounter during the working day. There are fewer workers, but managers require those who remain to be more productive. One of the ways workers can show value is by solving a problem immediately without having to wait for someone in management to come up with a solution. The ability to apply effective strategies to solving problems offers a powerful tool for the modern workplace. Individuals with these skills are highly sought after.

Most pupils are not explicitly taught techniques for effective problem solving. Some students will acquire limited problem-solving skills indirectly as they do their assignments and project work, but well-developed problem-solving skills are critical for all students.

Recall the list of top ten skills needed for success in work from earlier in the chapter (page 15; World Economic Forum, 2016). *Complex problem solving* is at the very top of the list. Equipping students with problem-solving skills needs to be a top priority for educators. It must also be noted that students need the ability to solve *complex* problems. Solving simple problems is straightforward. They have a limited number of variables to deal with, and the information needed to solve them is readily available. Complex problems have many variables, and solving them is more difficult. Often the information needed to design a solution is not readily available or incomplete. Complex problems are the kinds of issues that people face in real life outside the school system. Equipping students with the skills necessary to tackle complex tasks will empower them for lifelong success. Therefore, we must ensure that the problems we ask students to work on get progressively more complex.

A significant amount has been written about structured problem solving (Fensel & Motta, 2001; Free Management eBooks, n.d.; Jonassen, 2000; Simon & Newell, 1958; Tarvin, n.d.; University of Iowa, n.d.). I have distilled the problem-solving processes that these experts discuss down to what I believe are its four essential steps. I call this process the *four Ds*. The four steps are as follows.

1. *D*efine the problem.
2. *D*esign the solution.
3. *D*o the work.
4. *D*ebrief the process you followed when you are done.

By following these four steps, anyone can develop an effective solution to any problem. It is critical that teachers become familiar with this structured problem-solving process so that they can teach it to their students. (I will explain the four Ds in greater detail in chapter 7, page 55.)

Problem solving is the most important process skill of the seven pillars because three-dimensional thinking is an integral part of the four D problem-solving process. Convergent thinking is required for the logical analysis needed to define a problem. Once a problem has been defined, divergent thinking is needed to generate the creative, innovative ideas for solving the problem. Bringing those ideas to an actual working solution requires convergent logical thought to make things work, to make logical connections, and to overcome obstacles. Metacognition is required in the debrief step when assessing the effectiveness of your thinking and identifying the positive changes that can be made to your personal attitude skills and productive attitude skills to become a better problem-solver.

Another reason problem solving is so important is because the other six pillars of success process skills support it directly. Individuals need to have effective internal attitude skills in order to adequately produce working solutions to problems. When solving problems, students need effective information investigation skills to seek out and evaluate new information. Solving problems requires innovation creativity skills to generate new ideas for effective solutions. Because problem solving is often done with partners or in groups, interpersonal and interdependent collaboration skills are frequently important. After the problem has been solved, communicating the results in a manner that meets the standards of modern communication requires imagination creativity skills. Thus, problem solving is the pillar that ties the seven pillar process skills and three-dimensional thinking together. This underscores the importance of project-based learning as a teaching strategy. PBL is an excellent way to give students problems to solve and apply their process skills in order to arrive at a solution. Teachers should consider incorporating at least one PBL project per term into their instruction.

Conclusion

These seven process skills will empower our students for lifelong success because process skills can be applied over and over again in multiple situations. While the details change, the processes remain the same. Problem solving is the glue that holds all the other six pillar process skills together. The central role it plays makes it the ideal focus for teaching students these seven critical skills. I will explore the use of problems as an instructional strategy in the next chapter.

QUESTIONS FOR DISCUSSION

Please reflect on the following questions, either on your own or as part of a collaborative teacher team.

1. How much of your success in school was due to your ability to memorize? How much of a role does memorization play in the success of the students in the classes you teach?

2. How much divergent and metacognitive thought do you require of students in the courses you teach?

3. Are you consciously attempting to teach the seven pillar process skills when you plan your lessons?

CHAPTER 3

The Key to a New Approach

Now that we have discussed higher-level three-dimensional thinking and determined seven long-term process skills that students will need for future success, how are we supposed to teach students these skills while dealing with all the daily demands of teaching? It seems we are presented with an either-or situation—teach long-term process skills or deal with urgent daily demands.

Every teacher knows about the tyranny of the urgent, the all-important things we have to do every day—teaching what is in the curriculum guide to thirty young people who all have different learning styles and emotional needs and working with students who have special needs, communicating with parents and counsellors, and handling demands from administrators. On top of this, many teachers must deal with the task of preparing students for Department of Education standardized tests. Teachers are not given the credit they deserve for just making it through each day.

While daily urgent concerns consume a great deal of each teacher's time and energy, recent updates to the curriculum in many states and provinces now require teachers to also teach their students process skills such as I've discussed, like problem solving and critical thinking. The new K–12 curriculum for the province of British Columbia is one example of this (British Columbia Ministry of Education, n.d.b). The core competencies for thinking in this new curriculum are critical and reflective thinking involving analyzing and critiquing, questioning and investigating, designing and developing, and reflecting and assessing as well as creative thinking involving creating and innovating, generating and incubating, and evaluating and developing (British Columbia Ministry of Education, n.d.c). These are further defined for each subject area. In the curricular competencies for the new social studies curriculum, for example,

29

students are required to "ask questions, make inferences, and draw conclusions about the content and features of different types of sources," as well as "make value judgments about events, decisions, or actions, and suggest lessons that can be learned" (British Columbia Ministry of Education, 2019). These changing standards allow teachers greater opportunity than ever before to adapt their teaching practices to include new and improved instructional strategies.

Most teachers know that students need new skills for a changing world, but they feel they already have their hands full with everyday matters. If we are to be successful at fostering higher-level thinking and developing long-term process skills in students, then we must find a method of instruction that will allow students to learn higher-level thinking and long-term process skills *at the same time* as they are learning the required course content.

This chapter will elaborate on the key to the problems-first teaching approach—presenting the curriculum as a problem to be solved, rather than content to be told. It will discuss how posing content in the form of problems enables student discovery and engagement, ownership over their work, and eventually independence. Finally, it will discuss the implications of assessing this method and the results that have been seen thus far.

The Curriculum as a Problem to Be Solved

How can we move instruction away from the traditional teaching as telling, learning as listening method of instruction and implement a new approach that fosters discovery learning while still enabling teachers to cover the content in the curriculum guide? My answer is to present the curriculum to students in the form of a problem that they need to solve.

Problems make students think at a high level. Recall Progressing to the Highest Levels of Learning in chapter 1 (figure 1.2, page 12). You will notice that solving problems is at the highest level of cognitive function. Further, chapter 2 (page 15) explained that problem solving is the most important process skill of the seven pillars because it incorporates three-dimensional thinking as well as the other six process skills necessary for success. By cleverly crafting a problem to meet the specifications of the curriculum, teachers indirectly guide students into discovering the material that they would have taught to students using the traditional teaching as telling, learning as listening instructional approach. I will demonstrate the crafting of problems and the method for delivering the curriculum as a problem-based project in part two (page 37).

Problems initiate a progression that leads to student independence. The progression from problems to independence is illustrated in figure 3.1. Implementing the kind of problem-based learning that leads to this progression could be called the *teaching as facilitating, learning as discovery* method.

Problems are like puzzles that naturally engage a person's interest. Have you ever walked into someone's home where pieces of a jigsaw puzzle are laid out on a table? I have always been amazed by how a jigsaw puzzle piques people's curiosity. People gravitate to the puzzle pieces on the table and begin working on completing the picture. Something about the unfinished state of the puzzle draws people into finding the missing pieces. Problems, like puzzles, stimulate curiosity and draw people into finding a solution.

Trying to find a missing puzzle piece prompts the seeker to ask him- or herself *questions*: What is the shape of the missing piece? What colors are on it? Similarly, encountering a real-world problem immediately brings questions to mind: What is causing this problem? How can I address or amend this cause? What are the specific attributes of a solution to this problem? What resources are available? And so on. This questioning leads to discovery of the answers one needs to successfully develop a solution.

Discovery is vitally important to higher-level learning. Look again at the diagram, Progressing to the Highest Levels of Learning, in chapter 1 (figure 1.2, page 12). You can see that thinking and learning progress to higher levels when there is a significant shift to a student-centered approach that facilitates students becoming active in discovery-based learning experiences (Sayre, 2013).

A valuable byproduct of questioning and discovery is *interest*. Discovery learning naturally engages students in learning experiences. Architect and graphic designer Richard Saul Wurman (1989) underscores the central role of interest in learning:

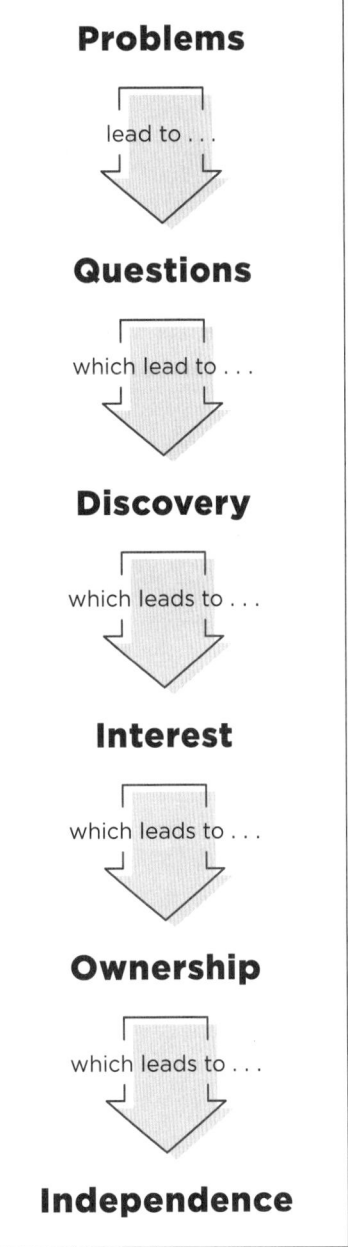

Figure 3.1: The progression from problems to independence.

> Learning can be seen as the acquisition of information, but before it can take place, there must be interest; interest precedes learning. In order to acquire and remember new knowledge, it must stimulate your curiosity in some way. (p. 20)

See *Loving What They Learn* by Alexander McNeece (2020) for more on the importance of interest in learning.

Problems also give learning meaning and interest by placing it within a larger context. This creates the framework necessary for optimizing the formation of long-term memories and results in *Velcro learning*, a term based on Richard Saul Wurman's (1989) idea that information without interest is like having only one side of a piece of Velcro. In Velcro learning, course content combined with meaningful context for the learner engages him or her in learning new material, causing the learning to stick in the learner's mind.

Problems are a wonderful way to shift the *ownership* of learning to the student. By not telling students the information they need to solve a problem, the responsibility for discovering the required material falls to the student. By giving students problems to tackle, we equip them with process skills that will empower them to solve not only the assigned problem but also other problems they will encounter when they leave the school system. We want students to become independent learners and problem-solvers so they can step seamlessly from our classes into the world outside school.

Presenting the curriculum in the format of a problem to be solved has benefits for the teacher as well. Instead of having the pressure of telling students all the course content to be learned, teachers share their expertise as students need it when students require answers to questions which arise while they are working their way through solving the assigned problem. Assigning projects in the form of a problem allows teachers to direct students into the course content to be learned without bombarding students with telling.

For example, in a junior high school art class, instead of telling the students about how changing the dominant item in a composition changes the tone of the artwork, let them discover it. Figure 3.2 illustrates a problem that can be given to facilitate that discovery.

Authentic Teaching and Assessment

At its foundation, this new problems-first approach to instruction has the same major goal of producing productive people as the traditional approach, but it comes at it from a different angle. Grant Wiggins (1993) captured the thinking behind this new approach to instruction and assessment when he said:

> [Instruction must include] . . . engaging and worthy problems or questions of importance, in which students must use knowledge to fashion

> The teacher tells the students in her art class that they will be assuming the role of a graphic designer at a local commercial graphics company and that the teacher will be assuming the role of a client. The teacher starts the role-play by saying:
>
> "Good morning, I am the coordinator of a folk music festival called Folk in the Forest. The festival is held at the outdoor stage in Wilson Park, which is surrounded by large trees—hence the name. What I need you to do is create a promotional poster for this event. The poster should be hand drawn to create a down-home, folksy look and feel. The festival committee has had considerable discussion about what they want the poster to look like, but they can't agree on what should be the major item in the design. So I am bringing you three ideas to work with for the major item in the poster. One group in the committee would like the name of the festival to be the dominant item. Another group wants to feature a trio of folk singers with guitars. And the third group wants to make a single guitar the featured item. I need three sketches for the poster, each with a different dominant item. And to help the committee make the final decision for the poster design, I would also like your thoughts on which of the sketches creates the best down-home, folksy tone."

Figure 3.2: Example of a problems-first lesson.

> performances effectively and creatively. The tasks are either replicas of or analogous to the kinds of problems faced by adult citizens and consumers or professionals in the field. (p. 229)

Here is the reasoning behind this new approach to teaching (Mueller, 2018b).

1. A major goal of schooling is to facilitate students becoming productive people who can contribute to society economically, politically, and socially.
2. A major aspect of being productive is being able to perform tasks in the world outside school.
3. Schools must focus instruction on teaching students how to do the kinds of tasks they will have to perform in life after school.
4. Assessment of learning focuses on gauging how well students are able to perform those real-world tasks or simulations of those tasks.

This kind of teaching and assessment is viewed as being more authentic than traditional teaching and assessment because in the new approach, the learning activities in school mirror the activities students will encounter in the world outside the school system. The problems-first learning approach outlined in this book aligns with this reasoning. It inverts the traditional sequence of steps taken to plan instruction. Instead of starting by teaching the curriculum, teachers start by determining a task from the world outside school that will require students to develop higher-level thinking skills. They design the task to lead students into mastering the material that is part of the course curriculum. Authors like Grant Wiggins and Jay McTighe (2005) refer to this approach as *planning backward*. As Wiggins (2002) states:

> We call it backward design. . . . Before you decide exactly what you're going to do with [students], if you achieve your objective, what does it look like? What's the evidence that they got it? What's the evidence that they can now do it, whatever the "it" is? So you have to think about how it's going to end up, what it's going to look like. And then that ripples back into your design, what activities will get you there. What teaching moves will get you there?

The planning backward approach to learning emphasizes the *application* of knowledge rather than the traditional emphasis on just the *acquisition* of knowledge. Traditional assessment, accomplished via assignments and tests, cultivates skill in rote memorization and passive test-taking. The new approach to assessment fosters higher-level three-dimensional thinking as students do real-world tasks. Students develop analytical, convergent thinking as they solve problems both individually and in groups; they develop creative, divergent thinking skills as they generate ideas for innovative solutions; and they must develop reflective, metacognitive thinking as they self-assess their work as well as the process they followed to produce it. The new approach to assessment provides a more complete picture of a student's capabilities.

In an authentic teaching and assessment approach, the kinds of learning activities that students do are designed to mirror the types of tasks that people do every day in the world outside school. Here is a list of the kinds of things that students do in an authentic teaching and assessment approach.

- Solve real-world problems
- Form fact-based opinions
- Make recommendations
- Participate in debates
- Design effective visual communication
- Work collaboratively with real and virtual partners
- Read and interpret literature
- Write stories
- Do science experiments
- Make presentations to people outside the school
- Conduct social-science research
- Solve mathematics and physics problems that have real-world applications

Conclusion

The daily demands of teaching create a relentless tyranny of urgent tasks that make it very difficult to add anything new to a teacher's job. If we are going to be realistic in making changes to instruction, then we must find a way to teach students higher-level three-dimensional thinking skills while covering the required content of a course at the same time. I have found that presenting the curriculum to students in the form of a problem that comes from a real-world activity is a very effective way to do this. It begins a progression that generates interest in learning and leads to discovery learning and student independence.

QUESTIONS FOR DISCUSSION

Please reflect on the following questions, either on your own or as part of a collaborative teacher team.

1. Do you struggle with the dilemma of teaching process skills for long-term success versus dealing with the tyranny of the urgent daily demands of teaching?

2. How often do you give your students problems to solve? Have you seen a shift in student interest, engagement, or ownership when your students solve problems?

3. How do you assess skill development when you give problems to students?

PART TWO

Learning How to Create Problems-First Projects

In this section, you will discover how to create problems-first projects. Chapters 4 through 12 each introduce a step for you to take in creating problems-first projects.

- Envision a new role for the teacher
- Ensure that problems are first and teaching is second
- Establish a real-world link using role-play
- Equip students with the four Ds of problem solving
- Expand your view of the curriculum
- Elevate the students' level of thought
- Educate the whole mind
- Evaluate holistically
- Ease yourself out of the picture

As you progress through these steps, you will increase your students' ability to problem solve effectively, help them think at higher levels, and ultimately equip them with the process skills they need to succeed in life after school.

CHAPTER 4

Envision a New Role for the Teacher

Our aim should be to engage students in relevant learning that develops the higher-level thinking process skills of the seven pillars of success. To make this happen, we must move beyond using telling as the primary vehicle for instruction. This shift in instructional style means exploring ideas that will be foreign to many teachers. The initial response to new ideas for teaching is often to focus on how the new ideas won't work—to only see obstacles to implementing them. This is because we often try to make new ideas fit into the way we already do things, which is okay if the new ideas are just small tweaks to what we currently do. However, what I am proposing in this book is an instructional approach that is substantially different from the way most teachers teach, especially those who teach grades 6 through 12 and beyond. I strongly urge you to resist the immediate inclination to look for obstacles and instead consider this new approach in more depth. While it may seem challenging at first, shifting to the problems-first approach is not beyond the reach of any teacher. After describing the problems-first method of instruction in the next nine chapters, I will offer suggestions to help any teacher make the transition to this new approach to teaching in chapter 13 (page 117).

This chapter will discuss the new role the problems-first instructional approach creates for teachers and explain how it differs from the traditional role of teacher as teller. It will then delve into the new task of crafting problems.

A Critical New Role

In this new approach to instruction, I am asking teachers to take on a new role in the classroom, but one important characteristic of the teacher role does not change—the teacher remains the *creator of engagement*. This has always been and will always be the most important role a teacher plays in facilitating learning. But as part of creating engagement plus facilitating process skill development, teachers must also be the *crafter of problems*. As I have indicated, problems are the key to a new approach to instruction that shifts the onus for learning to the students. Creating effective problems that are difficult enough to be challenging for the students, yet not so difficult that they cause excessive frustration, requires careful thought. In this new role, teachers must become adept at crafting problems that will accomplish a dual purpose—developing long-term process skills while simultaneously preparing students for upcoming classroom tests.

We must make shifts in our mindset about teaching if we are to make the transition to a new instructional approach that addresses the curriculum while simultaneously equipping students with seven pillar process skills. We need to move away from focusing solely on the content in the curriculum guide. This does not mean that we don't require students to learn the information in the curriculum, but it does mean we must see the material in the curriculum in a larger context. We must see the course content as the vehicle that allows us to teach much more than short-term memorization of information and procedures. Course content provides us with the raw material for constructing meaningful problems that both equip students with process skills to serve them well in the long term and prepare them for tests in the short term.

This shift to teaching with problems is aligned with the thinking of some of the great minds in educational theory and practice (see figure 1.2, page 12). Problems facilitate learning through discovery. For students to learn through discovery, they must become active in the learning process while teachers step away from center stage. In every course of study, we want to move as much as possible away from telling as the main vehicle for instruction and move toward students participating directly in activities where they question, investigate, explore, and probe to discover new information and experiences.

Part of the skill in crafting effective problems lies in the ability to design the specifications for a problem so that it indirectly guides students into the content in the course curriculum. This guided discovery allows a teacher to give students more freedom to learn on their own while still having control over what information students will be working with as they solve particular problems.

A Goal for Every Subject Area

Not every part of a course curriculum is suited to the problems-first approach, but teachers in most courses will find at least some part of their course material that can be crafted into a problem for students to solve. The key is to begin looking at a curriculum through the lens of creating problems.

A Response to Resistance

Relatively few teachers will have encountered a teaching approach like this either as a student themselves or in their teacher training. Therefore, it is important to note that teachers will likely require practice to be able to develop their problem crafting skill. The important point to remember is to start small and gradually work up to larger problems that will require multiple class periods for students to solve successfully.

It is not only teachers who will not have encountered a teaching approach like this. Most parents will have experienced the teaching as telling, learning as listening approach in their schooling. Shifting to a problems-first approach can be disorienting for parents because it isn't familiar. Some parents (and students) may immediately become concerned about letter grades. I have found it helpful to send out an explanation to parents that outlines the goals of the new approach and how the problems-first approach develops long-term process skill development while covering the required course curriculum. I have also followed up with a parent meeting to let parents ask questions about this new method of instruction. I have found parents are very supportive once they understand the reasons for teaching this way.

Conclusion

Teachers need to teach course curriculum to students. In the new role I am proposing for teachers, this does not change. What does change is the way we look at the material in the curriculum guide. We need to see the course content as the raw material for crafting problems for students to solve. I will outline how to craft these problems in the following chapters.

QUESTIONS FOR DISCUSSION

Please reflect on the following questions, either on your own or as part of a collaborative teacher team.

1. What is the role that you currently see for yourself in the learning process?
2. Do you currently give your students problems to solve in the classes you teach?
3. How much training have you received on how to create problems for your students?

CHAPTER 5

Ensure That Problems Are First and Teaching Is Second

A powerful way to begin to adjust mindset to support an instructional approach that is based in solving problems is to ensure that problems come first, teaching comes second. This is the most significant change we can make to our teaching. I cannot overstate the importance of making the fundamental shift to *problems-first teaching*. It will significantly alter the way students learn new material, and it will force teachers to take on a new role in the classroom—the role of the crafter of problems (see chapter 4, page 39).

One of the major reasons for beginning a lesson by presenting students with a problem before giving any instruction is that this is the way people encounter problems in the world outside school. Just think about the way that problems in life often arise. You don't get up in the morning, try to guess all of the problems you might encounter that day, and then acquire all the necessary information and skills you need to solve these problems before you leave the house—that would be impossible! What really happens is that you first encounter problems during the day while doing a personal or job-related task, and then you figure out what information and skills you need to acquire to solve that particular problem.

We can mirror the reality of the outside world in the classroom by making sure that the problem comes first *before* any teaching on a specific topic. And instead of telling students what they need to know to solve the problem, we must guide them into discovering the necessary information for themselves. To do this, we must shift the focus of our instruction away from telling students about a topic and toward equipping students with an effective process for tackling tasks they have never encountered before. We need to present students with problems to solve, not information to memorize. Teaching with problems first is an excellent way of providing relevant instruction to our students. They not only begin to comprehend the empowerment that comes from mastering a problem-solving strategy, but also they begin to grasp the relevance this strategy has to their life outside school.

What the Problems-First Approach Looks Like

What does teaching with a problems-first approach look like? Figure 5.1 looks at how a teacher could craft the junior high social studies lesson that was described in chapter 1 (figure 1.1, page 10) into a problem for students to solve.

This social studies lesson takes the content from the lesson described in chapter 1 and presents it as a problem. It is important to note that it takes time to get students ready to tackle a problem with this level of complexity. Students will require practice getting information through a role-play like this, and they will require practice in note-taking. While this social studies project provides a good example of what a problem could look like, teachers beginning to use the problems-first approach would start with much more modest problems. For students who are absent for that class period, I have a student in the class record a video of me doing the role-play. I then post that video in a private YouTube channel.

After the teacher has presented the problem, students will have an opportunity to interview the problem-giver. It is during this question-and-answer time that students will nail down the specifications for the product that they must produce. When I introduce students to the problems-first approach, the entire class of students interviews the problem-giver. I have found that this helps all students to learn how to ask appropriate questions as they listen to what other members of the class ask. As students gain proficiency in question asking, I often do the interview with the problem-giver with smaller groups of students.

When we utilize the problems-first approach, we're doing more than giving students a chance to learn course content. By posing problems to students, we teach the seven pillar process skills at the same time that students interact with the content in the curriculum—content remains important.

Let's look at the Global Custom Tours project (see figure 5.1) from the perspective of teaching the seven pillar process skills. By giving students the bus tour problem to solve, the teacher is asking students to apply independent problem-solving skills (pillar 7). By only providing students with directions to follow instead of telling them the information they require, the teacher is helping students apply information investigation skills (pillar 2) to obtain the information they need to solve the problem. By having the students work with a partner, the teacher encourages the development of interdependent collaboration skills as well as interpersonal skills (pillars 6 and 5). The

> The bell rings, indicating the beginning of class. A social studies teacher begins the class by explaining the following.
>
> "Today you are going to be working as researchers for Global Custom Tours, a tour company that arranges bus tours and ocean cruises around the world. Remember what we have been discussing in class about the concept of value-added? One of the ways that Global Custom Tours can compete with other tour companies is in adding value to its services that the other companies don't provide. Global Custom Tours adds value to its tours by providing a customized informational service as part of its tour packages.
>
> "For this project, you are assuming the role of a researcher for Global Custom Tours. You have just been called into your boss's office for a meeting. I will be assuming the role of your boss. The meeting begins like this."
>
> The teacher begins to role-play the part of a boss at Global Custom Tours.
>
> "OK, here is the project I want you to start working on. Global Custom Tours has been approached by a group of high school social science teachers from Toronto, Canada, about creating a bus tour of the Normandy area in northern France for next summer.
>
> "They are particularly interested in the history of the D-Day landings during World War II, and, of course, they want to know about the landings of the Canadian troops and the challenges the troops faced. The teachers have asked for us to put together a pamphlet on the landings so their students can understand the historical context before heading out to the beach in Normandy. The pamphlet should be no more than eight pages in length. You'll need to include the relevant historical information, photos of the Canadian landings, and the sequence of events to show the progress of the Canadian troops on D-Day. In the pamphlet, you will need to describe to the teachers what happened to the Canadian troops over the course of D-Day, and whether they reached their objectives.
>
> "The teachers want to go out on the beach where the landings took place and retrace the steps of the soldiers so they can get a grasp of the difficulties the German defenses presented for the Canadian troops. The pamphlet must describe the Canadians' progress up the beach. The pamphlet should act as a guide that the teachers can follow when they are retracing the landing. Make sure that you fully explain any technical terms that are associated with the German defenses and the Canadian assault.
>
> "This is a pretty big job, and you don't have too much time to get it done, so I want you to work with a coworker to produce the pamphlet that will give the teachers and students the experience they have asked for. Remember that everything you produce for this project must adhere to the principles of graphic design and the effective use of color that Global Custom Tours follows.
>
> "Any questions?"

Figure 5.1: Example of a problems-first lesson.

students will have to use their imagination creativity skills (pillar 3) to create visually effective promotional material in the pamphlet. If students are asked to self-assess their work and what they did to produce it, then the teacher can address the development of internal attitude skills (pillar 1). In addition to covering the curriculum, the teacher is teaching both the seven pillar process skills and the full range of three-dimensional thinking.

It's important to note that not all problems will cover all of the seven pillar process skills. Even complex problems may address a subset of the seven pillars. Smaller problems may focus on only one or two of the pillars.

Benefits of the Problems-First Approach

The problems-first approach is compelling, perhaps most prominently because teaching this way forces students to be more active in the learning process. Rather than sitting passively and listening to their teacher tell them about the historical event of D-Day, as the teacher does in the example in figure 1.1 (page 10), students must actively participate in creating a solution to a problem. They become detectives hunting for the relevant information and expertise they will require to complete the project. The specifications of the problem guide the students toward the information they need as they go looking for the material to create the pamphlet. For example, will students learn about the crossfire created by the German guns set to enfilade the coastline? Yes, because their boss (the teacher, assuming the character of the tour company owner) has specified that all technical terms associated with the German defenses must be fully explained in the pamphlet.

As the students' roles shift with the instructional approach, becoming engaged and proactive, the teacher's role shifts also. He or she is no longer burdened with the task of teaching by telling. Instead, the teacher is crafter and presenter of a problem that facilitates student learning. The teacher can then get out of the way while the students get on with the task of solving the problem. That doesn't mean that the teacher now has nothing to do. Students will have questions that arise as they work their way through a problem, so the teacher will be a valuable source for providing those much-needed answers. The teacher will also have to monitor the students as they are working on a problem, especially at the beginning of a project and when students are new to this kind of teaching. Students may have difficulty getting started because they may not have had any experience with solving problems on their own. The teacher may have to make suggestions to get students moving in the right direction. The ultimate long-term goal is to completely withdraw from helping students solve problems; however, it takes time for the students to gain the problem-solving skills, organizational skills, and time management skills necessary to tackle these kinds of projects independently.

So the teacher can use his or her time to help students who are stuck by asking them questions or making suggestions for their next step.

Thus, once the teacher presents the task, the teacher's role shifts from being the source of all information in the classroom to that of a resource or a guide for students. To gain understanding of a topic or competency on a task, students can ask the teacher to teach them a traditional lesson, but they can also learn from any other source they want. They could search the internet, watch a YouTube video, or read a book, or they could even ask their parents or someone in the community for what they need. In this way, there is differentiated learning in the classroom that honors the different learning styles of each individual student. The role of the teacher shifts from being provider of content to facilitator of the learning process.

Framing curriculum content in the context of real-world problems creates a situation that ensures students take the lead in their learning, but it also has another benefit. It puts students in a discovery learning activity that is much more interesting and more relevant than learning by listening. Stimulating student interest is paramount in facilitating learning. Further, an additional benefit of using the problems-first approach is the shift of ownership of the learning from the teacher to the students. If we want students to be prepared for success in the world they will face when they graduate, we must get them accustomed to solving problems without the assistance of others. It is critical that we encourage students to take responsibility for their own learning. Teaching with a problems-first approach is an excellent way to foster this kind of independence.

It is important to note that the focus in a problems-first instructional approach is on *solving the problem*. Learning the curriculum content is incidental to the process of solving the problem. If the teacher crafts the specifications of the problem cleverly, the students will naturally encounter the course content that the curriculum requires for a particular topic. Additionally, the context of the problem will add meaning to the details that the students discover, making it easier for them to remember course content for summative assessments like written tests.

The specifications of the problem lead students into the desired learning. More importantly, posing the course content as a problem to be solved rather than just content to be memorized creates a context for the new information that gives meaning to learning the content of the curriculum.

Conclusion

The problems-first approach significantly alters the learning experience for students accustomed to the teaching as telling, learning as listening approach because they become active in the learning process. Students must come up with a solution to a problem as they interact with the content in the curriculum for a course they are taking. Consequently, students must investigate for relevant material, assess its significance, make connections to other things they have discovered, and form fact-based opinions and judgments from what they have learned in their research. In other words, they are actively creating their learning experience. This puts them right at the top of the progression of thinking and learning found in figure 1.2 (page 12). In a problems-first approach, students learn a whole lot more than just course content, and yet they still learn course content, just more comprehensively.

One key part of presenting content as a problem to solve is role-play. We will discuss the intricacies and importance of role-play in the problems-first teaching method in the next chapter.

QUESTIONS FOR DISCUSSION

Please reflect on the following questions, either on your own or as part of a collaborative teacher team.

1. Consider the lesson the social studies teacher gives in this section. How does the teacher ensure students are responsible for their learning? How does the role of the teacher shift in this lesson?
2. Discuss how the lesson facilitates discovery learning.
3. Look at the curriculum of a course you teach. Can you see an area in the course content that you could present to students as a problem to solve?

CHAPTER 6

Establish a Real-World Link Using Role-Play

Shifting your instruction to a problems-first approach gives students a taste of what life will be like when they leave school. An essential part of the problems-first approach, therefore, is creating problems that are set in real-world scenarios. By striving for a real-world connection with the tasks we design for our students to complete, students develop skills that will transfer to their lives outside of school.

Not only is the problems-first approach an effective way of preparing students for life, it is also an effective way to engage them in the work teachers assign to them. Students seem to sense immediately whether a problem may connect to the world beyond school, especially when they must take on real-world roles to solve that problem. In my classes, I ask students to be journalists working for a magazine, graphic designers working for a website company, biologists working for a government agency, and many other roles as they do their assignments. I have found that students enjoy trying on real-world roles. To make the scenario even more real, I role-play a real-world person when presenting the task to the students. I pretend to be a boss or client coming to the students with a problem that I need the students to solve in the roles I have asked them to assume for the project.

Benefits of Role-Play in the Problems-First Approach

Using role-play has four significant benefits for teachers and students: (1) elevating tasks to the highest levels of thinking, (2) shifting ownership of the problem from the teacher to the students, (3) requiring students to develop real-world communication skills, and (4) allowing students to develop their interviewing and questioning abilities.

First, as you will see when you refer to the diagram Progressing to the Highest Levels of Learning (see figure 1.2, page 12), solving real-world problems or simulations of those problems is a task at the highest level of thought and learning. Doing so gives students a chance to think and learn at this high level.

Second, when the teacher is interacting with students in character in a role-play scenario, students are unable to access the expertise of the teacher as *teacher*. If I have introduced myself as Mr. Williams who owns a local hardware store, then students can't ask me questions that only Mr. McCain can answer. In my role-play character as Mr. Williams, all I know is the hardware business. When students no longer have access to my teacher knowledge, they quickly realize that they must think for themselves. This shifts the ownership of the problem to the students. It removes the safety net by which students rely on me to give them the answers to their questions. This is an excellent way to develop independence in students. The teacher won't be around as a resource for students to lean on when they leave school, so it is critical that students get accustomed to solving problems on their own while still in school.

Third, students must develop real-world communication skills to interact effectively with the in-character teacher during role-play. When I am pretending to be their boss, students get practice in how to interact with an adult in a work environment, and this practice sets them up for the same types of interactions outside of school.

Fourth, role-playing a character allows the teacher to discern students' abilities to find the information they need to solve the problem, and thus progressively withhold more and more information from students when they present subsequent problems. This helps students progress in their interviewing and questioning abilities. For example, when students are initially learning how to ask the problem-giver role-play character for information during the interview stage, they often get sidetracked and focus on minor details. I let them do this, but when I come back as Mr. McCain, I ask them about their session with the teacher role-play character.

> *"I understand you met with Mr. Williams and learned that he wants a website. How did that go? OK, now what content does he want on the site? What color scheme does he want? Does his company have a logo?"*

If they forgot to ask the problem-giver character about the content, the color scheme, or any other important details, then I use that as a springboard into a discussion with the students about how to ensure they always ask about important details. We brainstorm about strategies they could use to make that happen. We discuss the use of tools like checklists. As students progress in their question-asking skills, I will, in my role as a character, begin to give them misleading information to try to get them sidetracked. It is the students' job to perceive when the discussion is straying off course and to get the conversation back on track. It is the students' job as problem-solvers to ensure they get all the information from the problem-giver that they require to complete their task.

An Example of Role-Play in the Problems-First Approach

What does developing real-world experience using role-play look like? We have already seen one example in figure 5.1 (page 45). In that situation, the students worked for Global Custom Tours, and the teacher role-played the character of their boss. Figure 6.1 presents another example for a junior high school science class learning about the water cycle. In this scenario, the students will be working for a government agency. This problem will give you another example of how role-play can be used to bring a real-world experience to the classroom.

The teacher begins the class by saying:

"Today, I want you to be biochemists working for the government's Department of the Environment. You have just been called into a meeting with your boss. I will be assuming the role of your supervisor."

The supervisor begins the meeting as follows.

"I don't care what you are working on right now—drop it. I have something that must be dealt with immediately. Last month, we got a phone call from a man living in the Wingate district, a farming area just north of town. He reported that fish had died in Chekamay Creek after a heavy rainfall. Unfortunately, that phone message got erased, and we never responded to this man.

"Well, there was another heavy rainfall in Wingate earlier this week, and more fish in the Chekamay Creek died. This time, however, the man went to the TV station with his story, and some media companies have picked it up. This makes us look pretty bad, so I need to get the mystery of the dead fish solved right away.

"Yesterday, I had Jessica go out to Chekamay Creek and take a sample of the water for analysis, but Jessica had to leave town this morning. So, I need you to take over because you have the expertise to analyze this information. Jessica interviewed some of the farmers in the area who are currently preparing the fields for planting, and I will give you her notes. I will also give you this report from the lab's analysis of the water—it turns out the water contains high levels of ammonium nitrate, which is causing the fish to die.

"I need you to tell me what ammonium nitrate is and give me your best guess as to how it got in that water. And I need your ideas for how to prevent such high concentrations of ammonium nitrate from occurring in Chekamay Creek again.

"Any questions?"

One of the students asks, "Can we get the TV station to explain what happened in our office?"

The teacher, in role-play as the problem-giver, replies, "No, that would be embarrassing for the department. Plus, we don't want to talk to the media until we know what is causing the fish to die."

Figure 6.1: Role-play scenario for a problems-first approach in a science class.

continued →

> Another student asks, "Was anything else found in the water?"
>
> The problem-giver replies, "Just the normal things you would expect. I will provide you with a copy of the lab analysis."
>
> Another student asks, "What are the farmers doing to prepare their fields for planting?"
>
> The problem-giver replies, "They are fertilizing before they plant their seeds."

Figure 6.1 (page 51) shows how the teacher remains in the role-play character while the students ask their initial questions. The teacher transitions back to being him- or herself, their teacher, when students have asked all their questions of the problem-giver. After the students discuss the problem with the teacher, it may become necessary for the teacher to revert back to the role of the problem-giver in order for the students to obtain more information. Another strategy is for students to send an email message to the problem-giver (i.e., the teacher's email address) to get the additional information they need.

Starting Small

The examples in figures 5.1 (page 45) and 6.1 (page 51) are more complex problems that a teacher must build up to for students to be able to tackle them successfully. Teachers need practice as well, both in crafting problems and in presenting the projects as a role-play. To build confidence for both the students and the teacher, I suggest starting with much more modest problems. Figure 6.2 presents an example of a very modest problem for a middle school science class.

> The teacher begins the class by saying:
>
> "For this project, I want you to imagine that you are working for the local library. You are about to be called into a meeting with the head librarian. I will be playing the role of the head librarian."
>
> The librarian begins the meeting as follows.
>
> "As you may know, the library will be hosting a week-long event on how energy is used in our city. The event planning committee has asked us to set up a number of displays that demonstrate some aspect of energy. One of the displays they want is a simple electrical circuit with a light and a switch powered by a battery. I don't know very much about electrical circuits, so I need you to set up this display. The event committee has asked a local lighting store to bring us the wire, switch, light, and battery that will be needed. I need you to figure out how to set it up.
>
> "Any questions?"

Figure 6.2: A small problems-first project.

A problem like this can easily be solved in a normal class period. It does not ask too much of the students, nor does it require a lot of "acting" by the teacher. However, by putting the lesson in the form of a problem with real-world roles for the students and the teacher, it does shift the traditional roles in the classroom significantly. The onus is on the students to come up with a solution. The teacher becomes a guide and valuable source of information for the students as they tackle the task.

Transitioning to the problems-first instructional approach is much easier if a teacher starts with a number of small problems. This gives both the teacher and the students practice with the new teaching method so they can adjust to the new roles in the classroom.

Conclusion

One of the benefits of using a role-play strategy is that the roles assumed by the students and the teacher give young people practice in what it is like to be in a real-world position while they are still in school. I have found that students quickly recognize the relevance of this kind of learning experience to their future lives outside school.

QUESTIONS FOR DISCUSSION

Please reflect on the following questions, either on your own or as part of a collaborative teacher team.

1. What resources are available to you that will give you information on the kinds of things people do in jobs outside the school system?

2. Look at the curriculum of a course you teach. Is there a real-world product (memo, video, graphic art, presentation, model, food item, piece of furniture, or something similar) that students could produce for part of the course? Who in the real world would produce that product in their job?

3. Create a scenario in which the students take on that role to produce the product you have identified.

CHAPTER 7

Equip Students With the Four Ds of Problem Solving

As I have mentioned, independent problem solving (pillar 7) is the dominant process skill because it binds all the other process skills together. The importance of learning how to solve problems cannot be overstated. It provides a backbone that connects and facilitates the application of three-dimensional thinking and the other six process skills. If you had to choose just one of the seven pillar process skills to focus on, then this is the one to choose. If you are implementing a problems-first teaching approach, students will need to be equipped with an effective problem-solving strategy to operate successfully in a different learning environment.

How do you solve a problem effectively, especially a problem that you have never seen before? The key is to employ a structured process that empowers you to come up with the required solution. This process provides you with a road map to follow even when you are confronted with a new kind of problem. It is essential that every student learns how this process can be applied to any kind of problem—personal, interpersonal, or work-related.

I developed the structured problem-solving process that I teach by distilling the problem-solving process to the minimum number of steps necessary to create effective solutions. I call this problem-solving strategy the *four Ds* (see figure 7.1, page 56).

The four Ds are (1) define, (2) design, (3) do, and (4) debrief. We will discuss each of these in the following sections. (Please note: The following descriptions of the four Ds go into a great deal of detail for those teachers who are presenting students with challenging problems at higher grades in high school, or even in postsecondary courses. Teachers who are just introducing the four D problem-solving process to students, especially students at lower grades, will not need to apply all the material outlined in this section.)

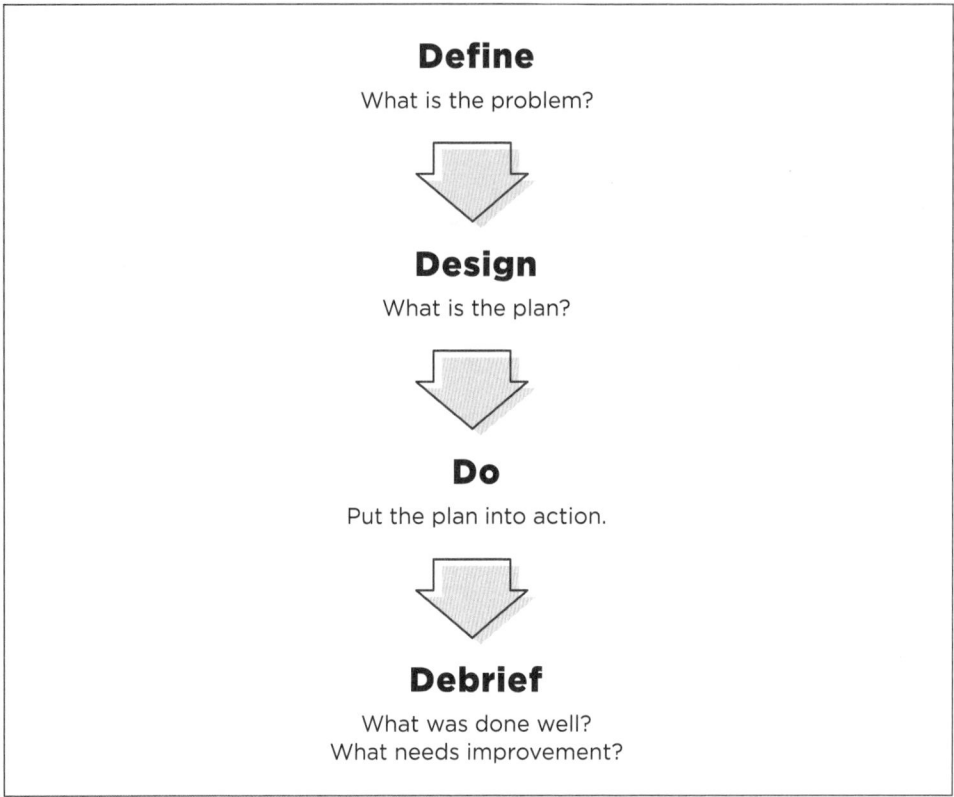

Figure 7.1: The four Ds of problem solving.

Define

You cannot develop an adequate solution without first knowing the full extent of the issue you need to address. This is why *defining* is a critical step in solving any problem. However, people often overlook this step in the rush to get results. Consequently, people often end up creating solutions that do not address all aspects of a problem, or they create solutions to the wrong problem entirely. For example, have you ever taken your car in for repairs and brought it home only to find that the mechanic didn't fix the problem? Or have you ever assigned a written project only to have a student hand in an essay on the wrong topic? In these cases, the problem was likely not adequately *defined* before work on the solution began. The work the mechanic or student did may be excellent, but it is not the correct work. The *define* step in the problem-solving process ensures that students understand all aspects of a problem so that any work they do to address the issue is the right work.

It is important to impress on students that they *do not* need to worry about solving the problem during the define step. During this step they should focus solely on finding out the full extent of the problem. I ask students to perform three sub-steps when defining a problem.

1. Capture the complete definition of the problem in a list of specific requirements.
2. Confirm the correctness of your problem definition before you begin work.
3. Know what's important before you begin a task.

Capture the Complete Definition of the Problem in a List of Specific Requirements

One of the aspects I love most about the problems-first approach to instruction is that I don't give away everything about a task by telling students all that they need to know. Instead, I outline a problem, and it is the students' job to find out all the details they will need to know to complete the task set before them. Students must learn to ask me for the information they require, or to find it from other reputable sources of information. They become the ones driving the completion of the task as they inquire about the nature of the problem to be solved, potentially developing real-world interview skills if defining the problem involves talking to another person.

The goal of an interview in this context is to develop a list of specifications that define the problem. In the world outside of school, the person outlining a problem often may have little or none of the expertise he or she needs to develop the solution. As such, he or she may not be able to state the problem in the technical terms those working on the solution need. For example, if a plumber with a marketing problem is outlining the need for a website, then he may not use terms that a web designer would recognize. Being an effective interviewer means being able to translate what a person says into clear, concise statements that specify all aspects of the problem in the technical language those who will be working on the problem use.

Once the teacher in the role of the problem-giver has presented the problem to students, the next step students perform is to interview the problem-giver to get additional information regarding the nature of the problem to be solved. Students must ask questions about all aspects of the issue to fill in any gaps in their understanding of the problem and acquire any details they may have overlooked.

When someone has a problem that needs solving, it is important to listen carefully to what he or she has to say because he or she may not use precise technical terms when explaining the problem. Often students must "translate" what the problem-giver is saying into wording that problem-solvers would understand. Some of this translation may occur during the interview, but usually the bulk of the translation happens after the interview is over. I ask students to quantify, as much as possible, both the current conditions and the work that the person is requesting. When students are doing this translation, I ask them to create a list of specifications in point form. (For an example of a point-form list, see figure 7.2, page 58, in the next section.)

Confirm the Correctness of Your Problem Definition Before You Begin Work

Communication can be a difficult thing. People often misinterpret what someone has said, or, instead of listening carefully, jump to conclusions the actual message does not support. These kinds of miscommunications can be disastrous for anyone trying to define a problem. Without first confirming that you have heard things correctly, it is entirely possible to work on the solution to a problem using incorrect information. Because there is a possibility of hearing things incorrectly, I teach students to confirm their understanding of the problem with the problem-giver—in this case, me—during the interview process by repeating back to me what they believe I have said.

With more complex problems, the need for confirming the definition of a problem increases. I ask students to begin by submitting a written problem definition for the problem-giver to review before they begin to work on a task. For example, the written problem definition for the Global Custom Tours task outlined in figure 5.1 (page 45) might look like what is written in figure 7.2.

Global Custom Tours Project

Overview

Create a pamphlet for high school social science teachers from Toronto, Canada, that will help them understand the landing of Canadian troops on Juno Beach on D-Day (June 6, 1944).

Specifics

1. Provide context for Canadian troops who took part in landing on Juno Beach using photos and other historical information.
2. Describe the objectives for the Canadian troops on D-Day.
3. Outline the sequence of events for Canadian troops on Juno Beach during the D-Day landings.
4. Assess how well the Canadian troops did in reaching their objectives on D-Day.
5. Create a pamphlet no longer than eight pages.

Figure 7.2: Problem definition specifications in point form.

Submitting a written problem definition is an essential step that prevents students from wasting time working on the wrong task. Confirming the task you are being asked to do is especially important in the world outside school since it protects you from clients who change their mind and blame you for not getting it right.

Know What's Important Before You Begin a Task

A contractor would not begin building a house for a property owner if the owner said, "I'm not sure which part of the house is most important to me and what I want it to look like; I'll figure that out when you're done." Of course not! The only way to determine where to focus your efforts on a project is by knowing what is important from the outset. In the same way, the only way a student can set priorities is by knowing what aspects of a project are most important and how they will be evaluated. However, often students have little idea of how teachers evaluate many of their assignments. The model they are used to is one in which they hand in work, the teacher takes it away and marks the work in secret, and eventually the work comes back to the students with a grade on it. One of the goals of problems-first learning is to change that. Therefore, I stress to my students they must probe to determine what the essential characteristics are for a project and how I am going to mark it before they begin working on the task. Determining priorities is a critical step to take in any real-world project.

The next step in the four D problem-solving process is *design*.

Design

The *design* step is all about planning. Good planning ensures a logical strategy for developing a solution, preventing a person from wasting time and effort on a trial-and-error approach. The person solving the problem must determine the best way to do the task considering the constraints of time, equipment, resources, and money. Time, of course, is the biggest concern for students while they are still in school. The goal of the design step is to create a formal plan that they can check and discuss with the members of their project team and with the teacher. Again, as projects become more complex, the need for a formal plan becomes increasingly important.

I ask students to create a written plan the first time they are given a problems-first assignment, so they get in the habit of making this document for each problems-first assignment they will do in the future. Figure 7.3 (page 60) presents an example of a template that students can use to document the design step.

Developing a written plan not only provides evidence of their thinking but also provides a document that we can look at together to check the logic of their thought process or to discuss the creativity of their proposed solution. Forming the habit of creating written plans equips students with a useful technique for effectively solving the increasingly complex problems they will encounter later in their classes and beyond the classroom.

There are five important sub-steps to *design*.

1. Generate ideas.
2. Create an overview of the solution.
3. Determine the knowledge and expertise you need to acquire.
4. Plan for the resources you will need.
5. Plan for managing your time.

Project Title: _____

Project Deadline: _____

Overview of Solution

Learning Needed to Do This Project

Resources Needed to Do This Project

Specific Subtasks With Intermediate Deadlines

Figure 7.3: The Solution Design Form.

*Visit **go.SolutionTree.com/21stcenturyskills** for a free reproducible version of this figure.*

For small problems, the need for using sub-steps may be minimal or may not be applicable at all. However, as problems become bigger and more complex, the need for planning increases greatly. Therefore, I get students to consider each of the following sub-steps when doing their solution design.

Generate Ideas

The first step in designing a solution to a problem is for the students to generate as many ideas as they can for solving the problem. There are two important parts to this.

1. Investigate.
2. Imagine and innovate.

Investigate

In the define step, students identify what they must do, but they do not yet have insight into the history that led to the problem. Neither do students, at that stage, know of other solutions that others have already tried, and they can learn a great deal from the successes and mistakes that others have made.

Imagine and Innovate

Now it is time to think about how to solve the problem. Students need to come up with original ideas for what actions they can take. Idea generation strategies include brainstorming, question asking, visualizing, and imagining as many possible solutions to the problem as they can. These strategies can be used with the entire class or with small groups. Students can start by trying to build on previously completed work on the problem. Can they modify or improve previous solution attempts? If not, is it possible to come at the problem from a new angle? Students can ask questions like: In a perfect world what would the solution look like? What would happen if this problem wasn't solved? What would happen if different people were involved? What would happen if the location was changed?

The great thing about the design step is that students are not encumbered with reality; there are few constraints besides time dedicated to brainstorming and planning. They merely try to generate ideas without having to worry about the implications in terms of resources or practicality—those concerns come at a later stage. I will expand the discussion on how to get students to imagine and innovate in chapter 10 (page 89).

Create an Overview of the Solution

The second step in designing a solution to a problem is to create an overview of all the tasks necessary to complete the work. Once students have picked, from all the ideas they have generated, what they consider to be the best idea for a solution to the problem, they must take the idea and identify the major tasks and subtasks they need to complete to make their chosen solution idea a reality. This overview creates a general road map to follow, and it helps students understand the scope of the work they need to do.

Determine the Knowledge and Expertise You Need to Acquire

Understanding the major tasks and subtasks of their proposed solution helps students identify what they need to learn before the work can be completed. Identifying what they need to learn in advance is a fundamental shift in the way learning takes place in the classroom. Having students, rather than the teacher, identify the knowledge and expertise needed to tackle a problem is a key to fostering student independence. It is critical that we increasingly shift the responsibility for learning from the teacher to the students to ensure they rely on their teachers less and less as they continue to tackle problems.

As students create the overview of a solution design, I ask them to make a list of questions they need to answer to complete their projects. When, as a teacher, I get together with my students to discuss their progress, I invite them to ask me questions they have about the learning they think they need to do. Getting students to ask me questions is a wonderful inversion of roles. Students become owners of their learning, and due to the clever crafting of the specifications for the problem they must solve, they actually ask me to teach them the material that I need to cover in the curriculum.

Having students identify what they need to learn empowers me to differentiate learning in my classroom. If the whole class asks the same question, then I can address the answer in a whole-class lesson. But if only a few students have a particular question, then I spend time with just that small group and let the rest of the class get on with their work. Because students are at varying levels of understanding, I begin by addressing the questions that all the students have. Once I have answered those questions, I move on to the questions that come from smaller and smaller groups of students so that other students can continue working. My goal is to teach students only what they ask me to teach them. Some students are better at asking questions than others. However, I have found that even shy students can make very real progress in their confidence in asking questions as they get practice doing projects that are presented in the problems-first approach. Although uncomfortable at first, this instructional approach shifts the responsibility for defining the task and designing a solution to the student, and it is this shift that creates the motivation, even for shy students, to engage in asking questions.

This approach also allows me to honor different learning preferences. Students don't have to get their learning from me. For example, if students are visual learners and they have found a YouTube video that teaches them what they need to learn, then they are free to pursue that avenue of instruction while I am teaching those students who prefer to learn from me. My role shifts from being the sole provider of instruction in the classroom to being just one of many instructional resources available to students. Please note: It is important that you equip students with the skills they need to discern credible information from noncredible before you encourage them to use other resources as a source of content. I provide guidance on this subject in chapter 9 (page 77).

Plan for the Resources You Will Need

As problems grow in complexity, so does the need for resources to solve them. Students may need to do considerable planning ahead of time to ensure that the resources they require will be on hand when they need them. Assembling resources can include arranging for training, finding and obtaining sources of information, organizing coworkers to meet for collaboration, and finding and purchasing necessary tools and materials.

Assembling their resources is when students begin to deal with reality. The ideas they generate for the solution to the problem may not be feasible given time and money constraints. This step may force students to return to the imagine and innovate steps to modify their solution and make it more workable.

Plan for Managing Your Time

Efficient time management becomes more important as the demands in life increase. Students have already experienced this as they progressed from the lower grades to the higher grades in school. Time pressure will only increase as their lives become more complex beyond the school system. Therefore, we need to teach students how to develop the ability to use their time wisely.

Again, this time management step is a reality check. Students may realize that they are not going to be able to implement their solution fully because they cannot devote enough time to the project to complete it before the deadline. This step may force students to return to the imagine and innovate steps to further refine their solutions.

When it comes to planning one's time, there are many tools and strategies available that students can use. I suggest begin by focusing on three tools and strategies for helping students manage their time as they work on their projects. These three strategies include the *task list*, *intermediate deadlines*, and *time planner*.

Task list is a strategy by which students create a list by referring to the overview of the project that was created at the beginning of the design step (see page 59). Once this list is complete, students can refine it further by ranking the tasks in decreasing order of difficulty or unpleasantness. Ranking is a very useful strategy for ensuring students use their time effectively. We naturally want to spend our time doing things we like and avoiding or postponing more difficult or uninteresting tasks, but it may be helpful for students to start with the most difficult or most unpleasant task first and get it out of the way. The task list helps them do this without feeling overwhelmed. Then the rest of the tasks can be done in decreasing order of difficulty or unpleasantness. It should be noted that while this strategy can be very useful, it does not necessarily apply to all projects.

The second time management strategy I ask students to use is the setting of *intermediate deadlines*. Working to complete a project to meet a final deadline is a fact of life outside school (inside school as well). However, setting only a final deadline is not an effective way to gauge whether you are on track for meeting it. It is much more helpful for students to set intermediate deadlines for the subtasks in the project.

Using a *time planner* is the strategy that allows the student to organize and effectively use the other two strategies. The planner can be paper-based or on a phone calendar, tablet, or computer. Electronic time planning tools have the advantage of having alarms that can be set to remind students of upcoming intermediate deadlines, meetings, and so on.

Once the students' solution is designed, the next step is to *do* it!

Do

Students have already used their imagination to think of creative ways to solve the problem. The *do* step is when those plans are put into action. The do step is when students begin the work of implementing a solution to accomplish something useful. Now they need to imagine how they can creatively communicate their thinking.

The product that students produce in the do step can take many forms. Students might perform in a play, create a sculpture, sing a song, build a desk, write a short story, cook a meal, improve a way of doing something, improve an existing item, participate in a debate, make a video, create a new innovation, do an experiment, write an essay, create a multimedia presentation, create a Photoshop image, or produce a digital visual effect for video, just to name a few of the myriad possibilities. The goal of the do step is for the students to create a product that best demonstrates the learning they have done to solve the problem. The teacher can evaluate the product in terms of how well it reflects the students' thought processes. The product illustrates the ability to define and design a solution to a problem.

It is at the do stage of the problem-solving process that students apply some, or all, of the seven pillar process skills to produce something that addresses the issues they identified in the define step. A well-crafted problem forces the students to identify what they need to learn in order to complete the required work. They apply their internal attitude skills to self-motivate, take initiative, manage their time, and persevere when they encounter difficulties. Students develop their interpersonal skills in the define and design steps if they are working with partners or in a group. In the do step, students further develop their interpersonal skills by interacting in interviews with resource people as they ask questions to get needed information. If the problem requires innovation of some kind, then in the design and do steps, students will create something new or improved and test it to see if it performs as they intended.

It is important that students see that the process of solving problems does not follow a linear trajectory. There can be considerable interaction between the design and do steps. Often the investigation done in the do step will cause students to rethink the solution they initially proposed. Rethinking the solution will take them back to the design step to revise some, or all, of the planning they did previously. This circularity can be seen in figure 7.4.

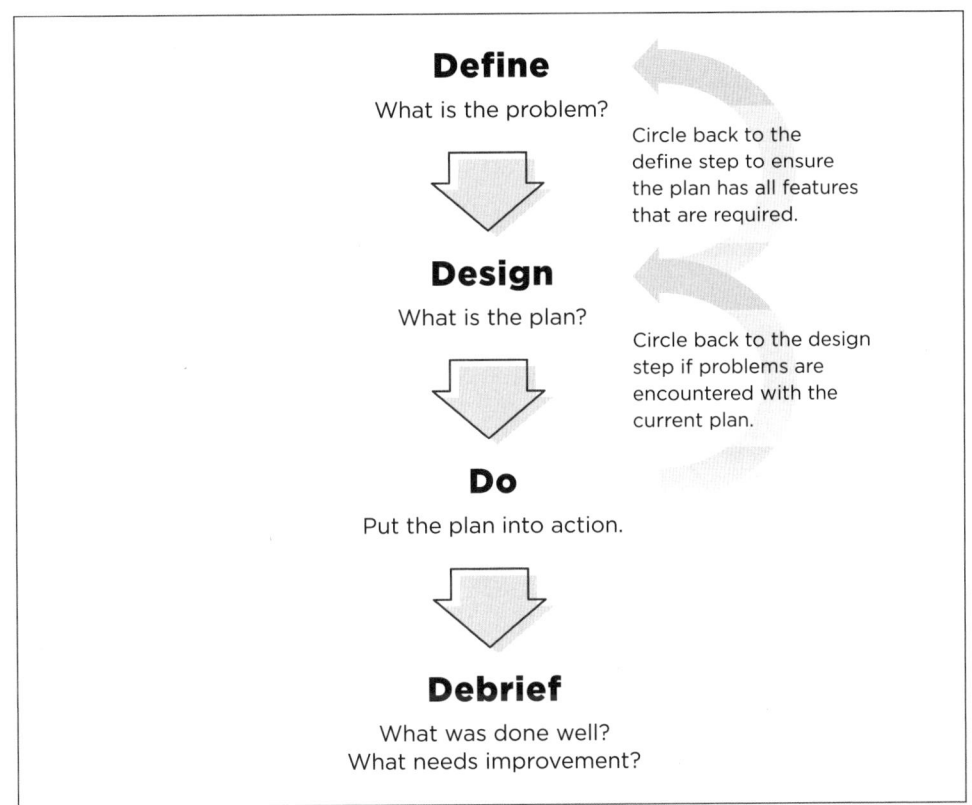

Figure 7.4: The circular process of problem solving.

When using the circular process of problem solving to work through solutions, students may realize that there are some flaws in their thinking. When they are putting their plans into action, an idea about a new way to imaginatively communicate their thinking may emerge. This could happen while writing a short story or drawing a picture or holding a debate or inventing a new product or service. Whether new, improved ideas come while they are engaging in the circular process or while putting plans into action, students will have to return to the design step to revise their plans. Teachers should impress on students that the circular nature of revisiting and revising previous ideas is an everyday part of creative endeavors. Circular learning is precisely what we teach students when we introduce them to the writing process. There is a circular nature to the plan, draft, and revise steps when students are composing written material.

The final step of the four D problem-solving process is to *debrief*.

Debrief

Debriefing involves revisiting each stage of the problem-solving process and reflecting on what one learned, how one learned it, and how the product or the process could be better next time. Debriefing, by its very nature, is a circular activity (see figure 7.5). It is vital that students understand that learning does not stop when they hand in a completed project. Some of the most significant learning happens *after* a project is completed by taking time to reflect on the work that has been done. In life outside school, constant improvement in your field of endeavor gives you a competitive edge.

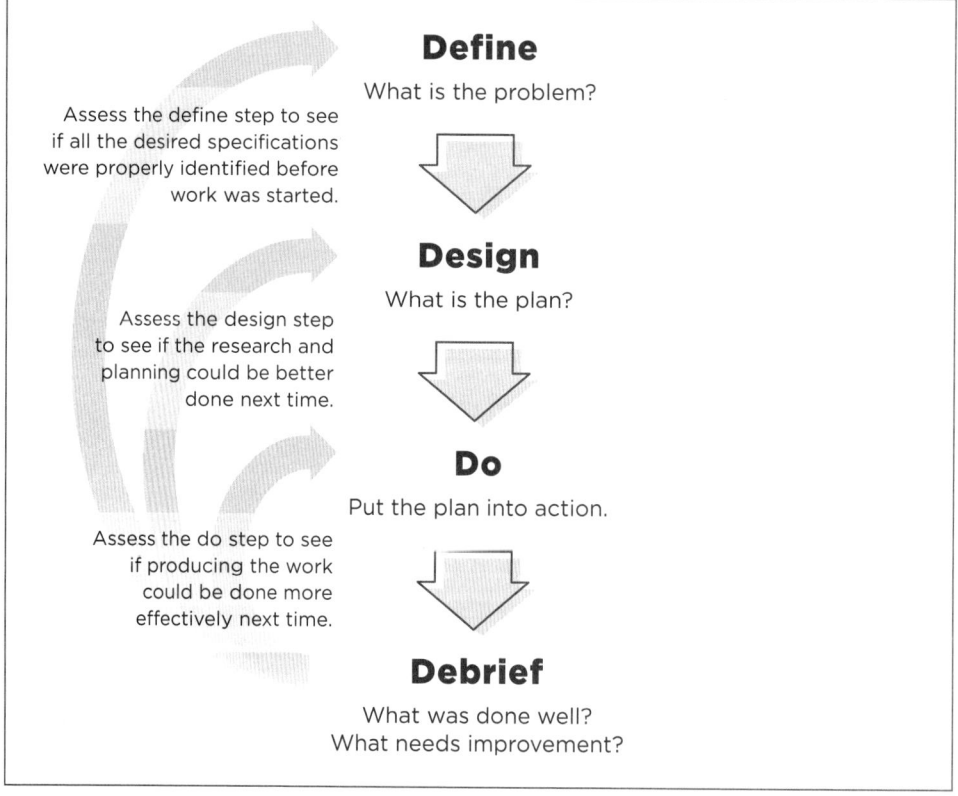

Figure 7.5: The key to the debrief step is circling back to reflect on what has been done.

Learning never stops. Once a project is finished, wise people revisit the process they followed to produce the work to see if it could be done better next time—in other words, to learn from their experience.

A sole focus on the product is not the best way to help students do better the next time they have to produce a similar product. If you want students to improve a product, they must also improve the *process* they used to create the product. A major goal of the debrief step is to examine the process that students followed while solving the problem. Initially, the teacher may lead the entire class or individual groups through this examination. However, the long-term goal is to pass more and more of the responsibility for this task to the students. This is in contrast with the typical linear process students experience in traditional teaching, which begins when a teacher assigns a project and ends when that project is handed in. In the traditional education context, students learn that their responsibility for an assignment ends when they hand it in because the teacher takes the work away, assigns a mark in secret, and then, usually without much discussion about how he or she determined that mark, the teacher moves on to introducing new material and assigning a new project. Not only does this create a linear conception of work for students, it also denies them the opportunity to learn from their mistakes, and it thwarts students taking ownership of their learning.

One of the major obstacles to student ownership of learning is that teachers do almost all the evaluation of student work. It is critical that we get students involved in the evaluation of their own work. I get students to go back to the define step to find the criteria for judging how well they accomplished the task. Since that criteria tells the students how I will evaluate them, they also can assess how well they think they have done. My role in assessment shifts to becoming someone who either confirms the accuracy of the student's self-evaluation of his or her work or communicates with the student about the gap between the student's and teacher's evaluations.

I do not stop at having students evaluate the final product of their projects when assessing their work. I also have students assess the methods they used when they worked on the project. This leads students into metacognitive thinking as students reflect on the way they went about solving the problem (Siegesmund, 2017). They identify inefficiencies so that next time they can be better when they have to work their way through a problem. In identifying areas that need improvement during the debrief step, students apply and develop their innovation creativity skills. Pinpointing areas of weakness and proposing ways for improvement is a major part of innovation. Getting students to examine their approaches and the procedures that they used to solve a problem naturally leads them to consider how they can improve their internal attitude skills.

With a thorough debriefing, the complete four D problem-solving process is complete and ready to be used again, with hopefully improved skills, for the next problem. The full diagram can be seen in figure 7.6 (page 68).

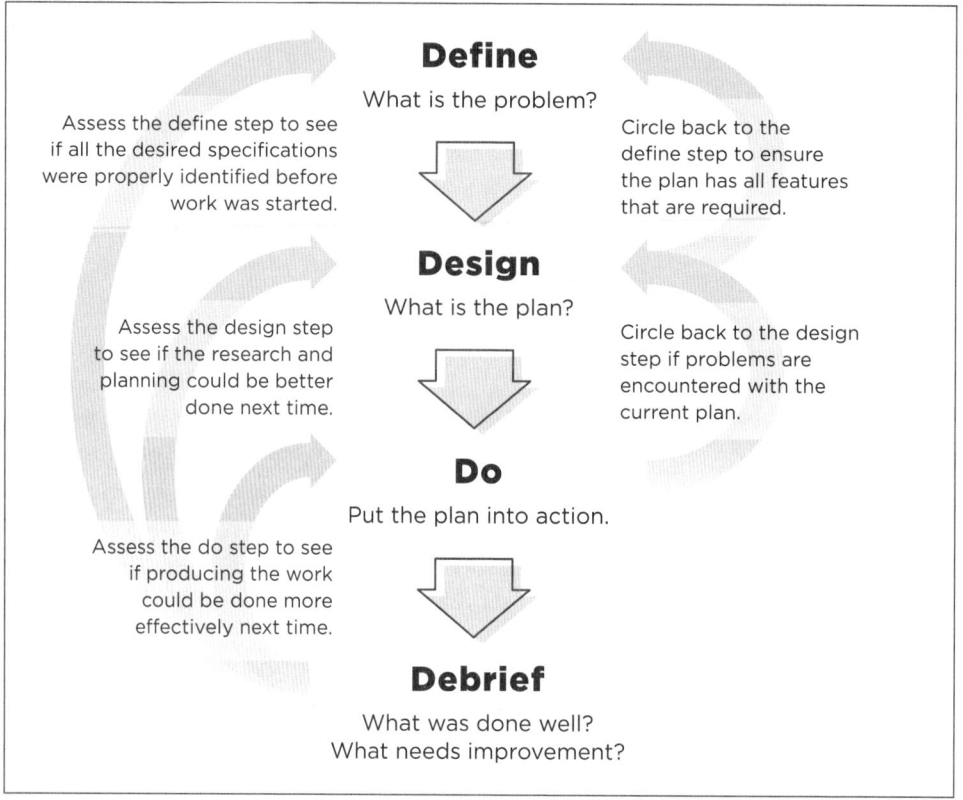

Figure 7.6: The complete four D process.

Visit ***go.SolutionTree.com/21stcenturyskills*** *for a free reproducible version of this figure.*

Conclusion

The four D problem-solving strategy can be applied to any problem in any field. Regardless of the subject you are teaching, there is great value in learning this approach to problem solving. The importance of learning this approach was confirmed for me by a former student who came back to see me at our high school about ten years after he graduated. He told me he had just been hired as the deputy fire chief for a local municipality, and the four D problem-solving process I had taught him when he was in my classes contributed significantly to his success as a fireman. He told me that he had used the four Ds in every job he had done in the fire department. For example, as the driver of a pumper truck arriving at a fire, he would begin by defining the problem by talking to the fire captain to understand the nature of each fire and by assessing the situation himself. He would then quickly design his solution for how to position his truck and run his fire hoses for maximum effect. Next, he would do the task by implementing his plan. Finally, when the fire was out, he would debrief his performance by assessing how he could have done things more effectively to learn from the experience. He also said that explaining this thought process had impressed the interview committee and been a factor in the committee selecting him for the position of deputy fire chief.

Learning the four D structured approach to solving problems will empower students for success when they leave school. It is essential that we teach this to every student who comes to school. I believe that learning the four Ds of problem solving needs to be elevated to the same level of importance as learning how to read and write.

The following chapter will discuss how to reach out and build collaborative, multi-subject projects with teachers across disciplines.

QUESTIONS FOR DISCUSSION

Please reflect on the following questions, either on your own or as part of a collaborative teacher team.

1. Can you see how the four D problem-solving process could be used to solve problems in your life, both professional and personal?

2. What kind of project work in your classes would require students to use the four D problem-solving process?

3. How could you structure the project work in your courses so that students would gradually need to use the complete four D process outlined in this chapter regularly in their project-based work?

CHAPTER 8
Expand Your View of the Curriculum

Early in my career, I attended an after-school meeting in which teachers from different departments were gathered to discuss the needs of a particular student. The teacher group determined that the student needed extra help with his writing skills, and they proposed that all his teachers encourage him in this area and help him with his written work. One of the science teachers objected, saying, "I don't teach English."

Of course, teachers can't be expected to have advanced expertise in all subject areas, but where does this notion come from that we only teach one or two subjects? The answer is that the school system teaches a compartmentalized view of life. For example, students learn science as a discrete subject quite separately from learning language arts, social studies, fine arts, and mathematics. Students can go from one discrete area of study to another with little, if any, crossover between them. However, this does not mirror the reality of life outside school. Many of the areas that are separated in school are often inextricably linked together in real-world issues.

This chapter will discuss how problems-first projects present an alternative to compartmentalized teaching, allowing for problems to challenge students across a wide range of disciplines. It describes one goal of problems-first projects—to create an open-ended problem with unknown possibilities for how students might solve it. Finally, it presents an example of a collaborative, multisubject problems-first project, to show readers what exactly this innovative approach can achieve through a simple problem.

An Alternative to Compartmentalizing

In school, we deliver a compartmentalized version of life. Generally, we don't give students enough practice in dealing with real-world, highly integrated problems. What often happens is that we teach theoretical concepts in discrete subjects and then leave it up to the students to figure out how to integrate and apply what they have been taught after they leave us. Many of the academically gifted students eventually figure out how to connect the dots and become successful in life, but many other students have real struggles making the transition into life after graduation. This needs to change. Subject material from all courses can be integrated by using a problems-first approach.

The key to introducing real-world problems into mathematics and science instruction is to use mathematical and scientific concepts in conjunction with other subjects. For example, mathematics and science can be taught together with English and social studies, writing and note-taking skills from language arts can be taught in science and social studies, and graphic design concepts from fine arts can be taught with almost any other subject area.

This will be a real challenge because in school we suffer from *hardening of the categories*. We have a highly specialized organizational structure in our middle schools and especially in our high schools. We have gone to great lengths to determine who teaches what. This is not representative of real life. To ensure school increasingly reflects the reality students will face after graduation, we need to make the projects we assign to our students broader in scope by including more than one traditional subject area in the assignment.

A Goal of Open-Ended Problems With Unknown Possibilities

Adopting this multisubject approach will not only expose students to real-world problems but also improve student engagement. Often the reason students are bored in school is because we don't challenge them enough. Instead of challenging students to exceed expectations, we often lay out the basic expectations we have for students at the beginning of the year by highlighting the minimums they need to pass. Instead, we need to establish a collaborative learning environment that conveys to our students that we will join them in exploring new material and learn together in the process.

Part of creating the collaborative environment in our classes means we need to shift away from assigning projects that are limited in scope with entirely predictable outcomes and begin to assign tasks that are more all-encompassing and open-ended with unknown and unpredictable results. As projects become broader in scope, they naturally begin to include concepts and information from multiple subjects, and they also provide opportunities for teachers to learn alongside their students. More complex projects that are open-ended encourage students to engage in divergent thinking as they imagine possible solutions to the problem. As they progress from the idea generation stage to implementing their schemes, students will engage in convergent thinking as they work through the logical challenges of applying their proposals to the problem.

An Example of a Collaborative, Multisubject Problems-First Project

What does collaborative learning look like? Figure 8.1 presents a problems-first example of a collaborative, multisubject project for senior high school. This project covers content in physics, history, environmental science, and indigenous studies.

The only way your students will be able to tackle a task like the one the following example requires is to have integrated instruction from several traditional curricular areas. This will mean that you will have to talk with the teachers who instruct other subjects.

> The teacher begins the class by explaining to the students that this afternoon they are going to be assuming the role of representatives of a real estate development business whose current client is the owner of a large parcel of undeveloped land on the outskirts of the city. The owner wants to develop a money-generating fun park at this location. The real estate development company has just submitted a proposal on behalf of the property owner to the local city council to construct a theme park, like a mini-Disneyland, on the land. The representatives submitted their proposal a few weeks ago and are now attending a meeting at City Hall to discuss the plan with elected officials and city staff. The mayor, to be played by the teacher, will chair the meeting.
>
> "Good afternoon and thank you for joining us here at City Hall. We want to thank you for your proposal for the land on Graham Avenue. It looks like an ambitious project, and we want you to know from the outset that we support the idea of a fun park in our city. However, we have concerns that we need to discuss with you.
>
> "We are concerned about the proximity of the project to a native archeological site that was recently discovered. We have decided that we want a plan for the fun park that celebrates the local Native Indian culture.
>
> "We also have concerns about the environmental impact of this undertaking. We need you to revise your plan to show how you will adequately handle water runoff without polluting local streams and rivers. We also need to see how the project will be energy efficient so as not to overtax the local power grid.
>
> "Finally, because of the difficulties with accidents that other theme parks have experienced over the last five years, we have concerns about the safety of rides you are proposing. We want to see proof that the two roller-coaster type rides you will be creating will be strong enough to handle the forces generated during the ride, and also that the rides have sufficient structural strength to handle the extreme summer rain, wind, and lightning storms we have in the area. We are particularly concerned about the roller-coaster rides.
>
> "So, while we are in support of the concept of this development, we cannot accept it as it stands now. We need you to rework the proposal to address these concerns before we will reconsider it for approval.
>
> "Any questions?"

Figure 8.1: An example of a multisubject problems-first project.

Reaching Out

Talking to other teachers about collaborating on a project can be a challenge. Teaching in middle school and especially in high school can be a solitary existence for a teacher. Once the bell goes for the first class of the day and the classroom door closes, a teacher can spend the rest of his or her time at school without talking to another adult. Many teachers have mentioned to me that they are used to working on their own and are not accustomed to including others in the planning of projects for their students. It may require some effort to overcome the regular teaching routine and reach out to other teachers to make a multisubject project happen.

Perhaps your school already functions as a professional learning community (PLC) with grade-level or subject-specific collaborative teams. This will greatly facilitate the development of cross-curricular problems. You will all have to work together to ensure that the problem and proposed project address all the outcomes in your curriculum guides in those curricula areas that inform the joint project.

It might be easier for elementary and middle school teachers to design real-world, integrated projects because they are accustomed to teaching more than one subject to their students. The challenge for those teachers is to break down the barriers between the subjects that exist in traditional teaching so that they can explore the possibilities for crafting integrated problems instead of teaching each subject separately.

Finding Common Ground

Once you have reached out to another teacher or a number of other teachers, you must find common ground on which to build your joint project. The first step is to get together to discuss the content of each other's courses. This discussion may be all that is needed to get a project going. However, it may be useful to have some resources to help you discover the areas in your courses that overlap. Stanford University provides one such resource that will help teachers discover common areas in mathematics, language arts, and science (Heitin, 2014; available online at https://ed.stanford.edu/in-the-media/finding-overlap-common-math-language-arts-and-science-standards).

Conclusion

Multisubject projects reflect the reality of the kinds of problems that people encounter outside the school system. Making the effort to reach out to other teachers to create these projects will result in learning that prepares students for life after graduation.

The following chapter will explore ways to foster higher-level thinking as students tackle problems-first projects.

QUESTIONS FOR DISCUSSION

Please reflect on the following questions, either on your own or as part of a collaborative teacher team.

1. Identify a content area in a course you teach on which you could collaborate with a teacher in another curricular department.
2. What are the obstacles that make such a collaboration difficult?
3. Can you use technology to overcome some of these obstacles?

CHAPTER 9

Elevate the Students' Level of Thought

The burden of trying to cover all the content in a course curriculum often thwarts a teacher's desire for pursuing lessons and projects that facilitate the higher-level thinking required for effective information investigation. The sheer volume of material, added to the demands of teaching dictated standards, can be overwhelming, making it difficult for teachers to put a priority on teaching higher-level thinking skills. The pressure to get through a curriculum so that the students are ready to perform on unit, end-of-term, and year-end tests can result in the *content trap*—when the amount of material in a course traps a teacher into viewing instruction primarily as content delivery. The teacher then becomes a dispenser of information and low-level procedures instead of being a facilitator of higher-level thinking. Students are expected to soak up as much material as possible in preparation for content-focused written tests.

I call content trap instruction *Dragnet teaching*, a name I take from the title of a black-and-white TV program that aired in the 1950s. *Dragnet* (Webb, 1951–1959) was a police detective show that featured Sergeant Joe Friday working in the seamy side of Los Angeles. Joe Friday's famous line when interviewing a distressed female witness, delivered in his deadpan style, was, "Give me the facts, ma'am—just the facts." Dragnet teaching is, "Give me the facts, kids, just the facts." The teacher dispenses facts to students in talks, lectures, and handouts as well as by directing students to material in the textbook. Students do tasks from which they are asked to report the facts they retrieve. They get a topic from their teacher that relates to an area of the curriculum, and then they start looking for information sources. The goal of this exercise is to produce a report that demonstrates that students have learned something about the topic.

A great deal of work can go into this kind of project. Students may create maps, draw pictures, download photographs, produce spreadsheets and graphs, or relay their findings in a PowerPoint presentation. The emphasis is primarily on the content rather than *thinking* about or making connections among content. Teachers may measure the level of effort students put into the project by the amount of material that students have retrieved.

The drawback with this fact retrieval approach is that a report is a simple restatement of the work of others. Students may do little, if any, higher-level original thought when producing a report. Students change the order of points and possibly change a few words and call it their own. Producing a report like this is especially easy today because of the wealth of information on the internet that students can access using Google searches. All a student has to do now is find a post that relates to his or her topic, select and copy the text, paste it into a word processor, change the title and a few words, and hand it in. In many cases, I have found that students have not even read the entire text in their submitted reports.

Instead of having students report the material they retrieve, we want students to *process* the information they find to gain new understandings. This quote, attributed to Albert Einstein, captures the essence of our goal for information investigation: "Any fool can know. The point is to understand" (Quotes.net, n.d.). Moving from knowing to understanding requires higher-level thinking.

The first part of this chapter will discuss the elements of higher-level thinking educators should strive to explicitly teach their students. It will then delve into a situation many students encounter when undertaking a problems-first investigation—the vast amount of potentially unreliable data they can access on the internet—and explain how this is a perfect situation in which to explicitly teach higher-level thinking skills. The chapter will then present the steps of the higher-level thinking skills of analysis, synthesis, and evaluation before giving examples of how these thinking skills may be taught in a problems-first approach.

The Elements of Higher-Level Thinking

What exactly are the higher-level thinking skills that students need? How do we teach them? Before answering these questions, let's go over the notion of lower- and higher-level thinking by reviewing Benjamin S. Bloom's (1956) taxonomy of thinking skills. Let's also look at the update to the taxonomy that Lorin W. Anderson and David R. Krathwohl (2001) completed to make the taxonomy more relevant for the digital age. We can see the comparison of these taxonomies in figure 9.1.

The goal is to develop students' thinking in the three higher levels of the taxonomy—(1) analysis, (2) synthesis, and (3) evaluation—when they are processing information.

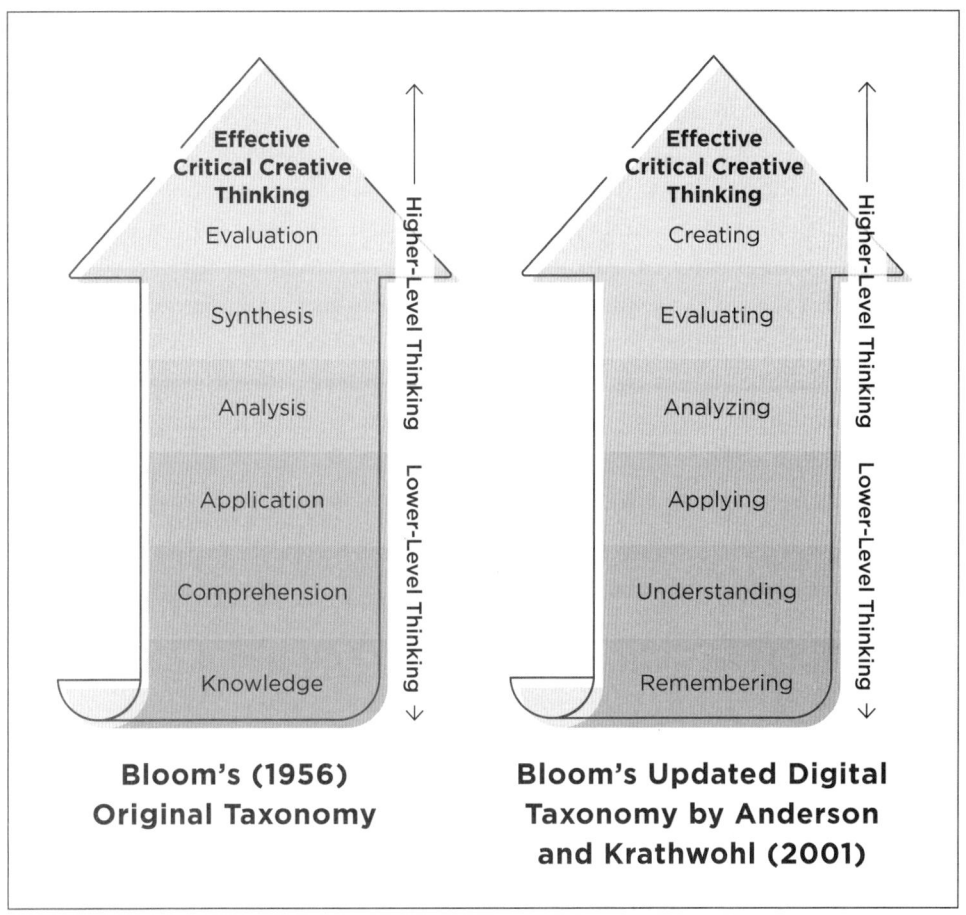

Source: Anderson & Krathwohl, 2001; Bloom, 1956.

Figure 9.1: Bloom's original taxonomy and Bloom's updated digital taxonomy.

I will focus on what students do after they find information they believe is relevant to the topic they are exploring.

The Problem of Unreliable Data

The internet has changed much regarding how we go about finding and processing information. Information today is not passive like it was in the past, when we could decide whether we wanted to engage with the information in a book or newspaper. Today, information actively intrudes into our consciousness. We must now deal with a deluge of data in our daily lives—Twitter, Snapchat, Facebook, Instagram, YouTube, text messages, email, phone calls, calendar alerts, pop-up messages, and a host of other information sources beep at us and pop onto our phone and computer screens, trying to get our attention with sounds, colors, and animations. When we go looking for information, the breadth and depth of online material available from around the globe is truly staggering.

Along with this astonishing amount of factual information, we are also exposed to the news—which sometimes presents facts of what is happening in the world but oftentimes includes ideas and opinions from individuals and groups whose views interpret facts rather than simply present them. Opinions can vary from provocative investigative thought to mainstream thinking to partisan political views to hateful and bizarre ideologies. Beyond news and news opinion sites, the internet also enables the average person to publish his or her views for a global audience by way of blogs, vlogs, and other means. A very short time ago, the ability to reach a global audience was only possible for large, well-funded news organizations, but due to the growth and sophistication of online digital tools, it has never been easier for people to publish their seemingly credible views complete with impressive visual design, graphics, images, and video.

The ease of dissemination that technology enables can create a problem for consumers of information because while online search tools have made finding information easier, it is harder to discern credible information and fact-based news and opinions from fake and distorted ones. Therefore, it is important that we teach our students to use higher-level, critical thinking, information investigation skills so that they are able to effectively discern the reliability of new information and use only that which is credible to form fact-based opinions.

In the following sections, I present a step-by-step guide for teaching students higher-level thinking skills to parse information they gather during the problems-first instructional process. I will present:

- The five steps of information analysis
- The three aspects of information synthesis
- The importance of information evaluation

Examples of these steps within a problems-first lesson will follow.

The Five Steps of Information Analysis

The first step toward developing critical thinking is getting students to *analyze* the information they find by asking questions about that information. Asking probing questions is a vital component of higher-level thinking. I advise students to ask the following questions when encountering written information in order to analyze the material before applying it to their own work.

Assess the Author's Background

Who wrote this? What are their credentials? Can you consider the author to be an expert on this topic?

Consider the Author's Subjectivity

What motivated the author to write the material? What is the purpose of this information—to inform, advertise, entertain, or satirize?

Look closely at the URL address. Is it trying to mimic a credible site? Does the author have a bias? Does the author have an agenda? Is the author trying to evoke a certain emotional response? What do links on the author's website or other posts he or she has made indicate about bias in the information the author is presenting?

Assess the Information's Believability

Is what the author saying based on facts? Are there sources listed for those facts? Are those sources reliable? Is the information up to date?

Check for Support

Is there backing from other sources for the information, ideas, or opinions being expressed? (It is best to have at least three sources.)

Apply Scrutiny

There are five steps involved in applying scrutiny to new information: (1) calculate, (2) correlate, (3) compare, (4) contrast, and (5) change context.

Calculate

Generate new numerical data or conduct statistical analyses based upon the information you have found that will help you see that information in a new way. You may choose to calculate counts, totals, averages, highs, lows, charts, graphs, tables, standard deviations, or other mathematical tests. For example, after retrieving information listing the budgets of the federal government for the past thirty years, you may choose to count the number of times the budget had a surplus of revenue, the number of times the budget was balanced, and the number of times the budget had a deficit.

Correlate

After conducting your calculations, ask, "What more can I learn from the information that I gathered if I rank, rate, categorize, and sort the original material or the new data?" For example, what can be learned if the political party that was responsible for each budget is attached to each of the federal government budgets, and then the budgets are ranked from greatest surplus to least surplus?

Compare

Can you find similarities between this information and material you find from other sources? For example, what similarities can be found if the federal government budgets are compared to those from another country?

Contrast

Can you find differences between this information and material you find from other sources? For example, what differences can be found if the federal government budgets are compared to those from another country?

Change Context

Translate your information to another context. Ask yourself, "What transfers and what doesn't?" For example, would your information have been valid twenty-five years ago? Will it still be valid twenty-five years into the future? If a person from the past came into today's world, what information about his or her life would still be valid, and what would not?

By applying the five steps of analysis to new information they discover during problem solving, students will have a much better idea of what their research is telling them. They will be able to discern if the information is credible or not. If it is not credible, then the material must be ignored or used as an example of fake or misleading information. If it is credible, then students can move on to the next step in processing the information: *synthesis*.

The Three Aspects of Information Synthesis

After discerning the validity of their researched information, we want students to *synthesize* their new understandings resulting from the data analysis to create deeper insights on the topic. This is where students use both convergent and divergent thinking to develop new interpretations of the information they have discovered. To help students with synthesizing information, I instruct them to follow three steps.

1. Look for patterns.
2. Predict something new.
3. Propose something new.

Look for Patterns

Finding patterns is essentially connecting the dots. Look for ways to reconnect, recombine, or rearrange what you have found to reveal something new about the topic. Generalize from what you have found to a larger population or category. Ask, "What happens if you link ideas together that were previously disconnected?" For example, does a pattern emerge when the amount of the surplus or deficit of the federal government budget is linked to the price of oil at the time the budget was introduced?

Predict Something New

Look for trends in the information. Extrapolate—make your best guess for what is next or what happened previously based on known information. Interpolate—guess what steps could have made it possible to get from one known point to another. Look for a progression or a process. Hypothesize imaginary scenarios—what if something was added or taken away? For example, based on the pattern of federal government budget surpluses or deficits when linked to the price of oil, predict whether the next federal budget will be a surplus or a deficit.

Propose Something New

Propose a new idea that resolves two or more opposing or contradictory thoughts. Devise something new to fill a hole in the information you have discovered, to meet a need you have identified in your research, to fix a problem that has become evident, or to answer a question or to resolve a contradiction in what you have found. For example, you could propose a shift to using green energy sources throughout the economy to stabilize federal government budgets.

The third and final step is to *evaluate* the information.

The Importance of Information Evaluation

We need to insist that students *evaluate* the information they have gathered if we want them to function at the highest level of thought. We can do this by requiring students to form opinions about what they have learned. They must then justify their positions using excerpts from their research. Expressing and supporting an opinion is a great way for students to add their original thought to a discussion. Teachers and employers alike highly value original thinking in the modern sea of digital information. We must encourage students to use the understanding they have gained from processing their gathered information to make value judgments on that information. In other words, we want to help students use higher-level thinking to draw conclusions and form fact-based opinions about the raw data they have discovered.

There are many books, blogs, and websites on the topic of teaching higher-level thinking. I encourage you to explore this topic further, but we can have an immediate impact on the level of thinking in our classrooms by simply asking students to form opinions based on their research. Here are some examples of questions and tasks that led to student research which also require them to form opinions based on what they have found.

1. Which country's policies have worked best in the War on Drugs?
2. Based on the kind of running you do, which of these six running shoes is best for you?
3. Which of these three animals is best suited to live in a desert?
4. Out of the Middle Ages, the Renaissance, or today, in which of these three periods in history would you like to live based on the following factors: political system, religious influence, working conditions, and access to education?
5. What is the best method for rehabilitating a stream contaminated with Eurasian milfoil weed?
6. Working in groups of four, decide the best location for a new youth center for your community.

Notice that the preceding examples all ask students to evaluate *two or more things*. This is important. If you only give students one possibility to research, then you are just getting students to produce a report. Evaluation requires *comparison*. Also, notice that each task requires more than just information processing. Students must make value judgments on what they discover. Crafting problems that require students to add this level of thought to their projects is essential when teaching students the 21st century information investigation skills they need to thrive in the communication age.

Examples of Higher-Level Thinking Within Problems-First Projects

So, what would a lesson look like if higher-level thinking is a requirement? One example, from a high school history lesson, can be seen in figure 9.2.

Does this project have the academic rigor needed for students to develop traditional information processing and communication skills? Yes—students will have to do research on history and geography to get the basic details for their stories. They will write two stories and an editorial. But will students have to do higher-level thinking to complete this project? Again, yes—they must synthesize the factual information they retrieve to creatively imagine the stories from the first-person perspective of the immigrants; in their editorial, they must do higher-level, big-picture analysis to compare the two stories; and they must form personal, fact-based opinions to evaluate which era's policies were better. Having the students create an Inspiration, FreeMind, or Mindomo file requires students to determine the main points in their stories and the connections to their research.

Figure 9.3 (page 86) presents another problems-first role-play for a high school science class that will require students to do higher-level information investigation as well as apply their imagination creativity skills.

The teacher explains to the class that the students will be assuming the role of writers for a magazine, and that she will be role-playing the character of the magazine publisher. The teacher informs the students that they, the writers for the magazine, are attending the regular weekly staff meeting to discuss the next month's issue. The teacher begins the role-play by saying the following.

"In the upcoming June issue of our magazine, we need something with punch in the area of immigration policy. I want you to write an article that will enlighten our readers about what's happening by comparing current immigration policies to policies in another era of history. I want you to organize the article into three sections, each with its own subhead—two stories from immigrants, and a final section written as an editorial. The first story should be a fictional account written from the perspective of an Irish family wanting to immigrate to our country because of the Great Potato Famine of 1845. Although your story is fiction, I want it to be based on facts, describing what the immigration experience was like. Your research should include details of the reasons why the Irish family decided to immigrate, the cost, and descriptions of their journey and their experience of landing in a new country. Also include detail regarding the process of gaining entrance into the country.

"The second story I want you to write is a fictional account of what it would be like if the same family lived in Ireland and wanted to immigrate to our country today. Again, although it's fiction, I want you to base the story on facts. Write both stories in the first person from the perspective of either the father or the mother. Keep the stories to about 750 words each. In the editorial, I want you to explain why you think the policies of one era are better than the other—you choose. Just make sure you justify your choice.

"We are going to publish this article in the hard copy of the magazine, but we are going to ask readers to respond online, so I want you to create a blog with three separate entries—one for each section of the article. That way people can respond to the content of each section separately. To help people understand the background for the two immigrant stories, I also want you to create a short video collage that visually captures the conditions in Ireland then and now. We'll put this video up on the blog.

"Now before you go, we have to discuss one other issue. I have been getting some heat from upper management about the lack of preparation by our writers. The bosses are concerned about the errors and poor research that are showing up in your work. I am going to need you to give me a plan I can take back to the people upstairs to show how you are preparing your articles. First of all, I want you to create an Inspiration, FreeMind, or Mindomo file that visually illustrates the connection of your ideas to the sources of your research. I'll need to see that file by Friday. Plus, when your articles are completed, I'll need you to get your work checked by someone else on staff before you submit it using the track changes feature in Microsoft Word. I want the Word file from you by the end of next week, and the blog and the video two days later.

"Any questions?"

Figure 9.2: An example of elevating the level of thought in a problems-first project.

> The teacher explains to the class that the students will be taking on the roles of workers at a nonprofit environmental society, and that he will play the role of the president of the society. The workers are attending the usual morning meeting. The teacher begins the role-play by saying the following.
>
> "As you know, for the last two years, we have been appealing to the local city council to institute a recycling program for the city. Well, at the council meeting last night, they finally scheduled us to give a presentation at the council meeting which takes place in two months' time. This is fantastic news, and I want to thank you for all your efforts that helped us to get this far. But now we have to finish this task. At the council meeting, we must persuade the council to actually institute the recycling program.
>
> "There are some constraints that we have to deal with. First, we have been given only ten minutes to present to the council. Second, if they decide to start a recycling program, they have indicated that the city budget will only allow for two types of materials to be recycled in the first year of the program. So, we need to come up with a presentation that will knock their socks off and convince them that starting a recycling program is the only responsible decision. Realistically, we will probably only have about six to seven minutes to do this because in the last two to three minutes, we'll have to make the case for which two types of materials should be recycled first.
>
> "You will work with a partner to create this presentation. We need you to make a strong case for the value of recycling. We also need you to figure out which two types of materials are the most important ones to recycle to begin with. We won't have a lot of time to give our presentation at the council meeting, so we need you to get your points across quickly. The best way to do that will be to represent much of your research graphically, using lists, charts, graphs, and diagrams to make your case for why recycling is important. We want you to use the same format when you make the case for which two types of materials the program should start with.
>
> "Any questions?"

Figure 9.3: Another example of a problems-first project requiring higher-level thinking.

This project requires students to do more than simply research and report on what they find. In this project, students must do higher-level thinking in order to meet the objectives. They must do their research and then present it to the city council in such a way that it persuades the council to start a recycling program. Then students must do evaluative thinking by deciding which two materials are the most important ones to recycle. Asking students to form an opinion based on the information they discover is a key to getting them to think at the highest level of Bloom's taxonomy.

Conclusion

Information analysis skills are crucial in the modern age of readily available digital information. In addition to the enormous amount of data to be analyzed, there is the problem of the unreliability of much of the information available. To process all this information effectively, students need the higher-level thinking skills outlined in this chapter. Teachers can even foster higher-level thinking by asking students to form opinions based on the information they have retrieved and analyzed.

In the next chapter, we explore how to foster higher-level creative thinking in the problems-first approach.

QUESTIONS FOR DISCUSSION

Please reflect on the following questions, either on your own or as part of a collaborative teacher team.

1. How can you use the five steps of information analysis with your students?

2. Where in your course can you ask students to apply the three aspects of information synthesis?

3. On what topics can you ask students to form an opinion on what they have discovered (and back that opinion up with what they have found)?

CHAPTER 10
Educate the Whole Mind

What does *educating the whole mind* mean? This is an interesting question that garners a variety of controversial answers. The popular concept of the whole mind is based on a somewhat faulty premise that has become widely accepted regarding the fact the brain has two hemispheres (see, for example, Pietrangelo, 2019; Pink, 2006). This concept arises from the notion that each hemisphere has distinctly different functions in the thinking process. Many have claimed that the left brain is that part of the brain that handles logic, analysis, and language while the right brain handles context, synthesis, and creativity (Pink, 2006). While certainly these ideas hold some truth, as our understanding of brain function grows, it has become clear that the distinctions between left hemisphere and right hemisphere do not accurately reflect the realities of how the brain works. Later research shows that brain function in thinking is far more complex than previously believed and both sides of the brain are involved in almost all types of thinking (see, for example, Jarrett, 2012; Lombrozo, 2013). In spite of this, the idea that the left side of the brain is logical and the right side is creative persists (Editors of Encyclopaedia Britannica, n.d.; Jarrett, 2012). Within the classroom context, much focus is often given to the logical, analytical thinking of the left brain.

A better way to approach educating the whole mind is to consider teaching the full range of three-dimensional thinking. Thus, for the purposes of this book, rather than thinking in terms of left- and right-brain thinking, *educating the whole mind* means helping students develop the logical, analytical thinking abilities of convergent thinking while also helping them develop the creative, innovative abilities of divergent thinking, as well as helping them develop the self-reflection that makes up metacognitive thinking. Any way you look at it, the point is that educating the whole mind means developing the full range of cognitive abilities, not just the logical thinking that is often the focus in the school system.

I highlight three strategies that teachers can incorporate into their teaching to educate the whole mind.

1. Encourage fact-based imagination.
2. Teach the entire writing process.
3. Enter the Idea-Storm Think Tank.

Encourage Fact-Based Imagination

Is it possible to encourage the development of imagination creativity skills while you teach students the content of the curriculum? The answer is *yes*! In fact, by sparking students' imagination, you empower them to remember content details much better than if they didn't use their imaginations.

So how do you get students to do whole-mind thinking across the curriculum? You do it by getting them to *tell stories*. When I say stories, I don't mean purely fictional stories that come solely from their imaginations, although those certainly have value. I mean *creative nonfiction*—stories that are fact-based, which students imagine after thinking about the research they have done. This strategy allows imagination creativity skills to be integrated into whatever subject students are studying.

Consider the movie *Amadeus* starring Tom Hulce (Zaentz & Forman, 1984). *Amadeus* is the story of the life of Wolfgang Amadeus Mozart. However, instead of presenting a dry examination of facts about Mozart's life and his music, this film gives us young Amadeus as a brilliant musician, but also as an immature young man with raging hormones and considerable arrogance. The movie also depicts an intense rivalry between Mozart and another composer, Antonio Salieri, as part of a plot full of human jealousy and intrigue.

Where does this story come from? The writer of the play on which the movie is based, Peter Shaffer, based the script on the life of Mozart, but his story did not simply communicate the facts of Mozart's life. Neither was his story a work of pure fiction. Instead, he looked for a story behind the facts. He used higher-level imagination creativity skills to create a narrative that combined the factual details together with his imagination to make a more coherent whole. You might not agree with Shaffer, but he presents a reasonable interpretation of Mozart's life based on known information, and the result is more engaging and memorable than a simple facts-only documentary.

We should encourage students to be like Peter Shaffer—to use their research as raw material for higher-level creative thinking. We must give them assignments that will help them use their imaginations to suggest the underlying story behind the information they retrieve. Requiring students to use their imaginations to play with raw research information helps them to become creative thinkers.

How does inventing a fact-based story like *Amadeus* foster creative, higher-level thinking? It does so because students must *interpolate* between the details of their research to connect the dots so they can create a believable story. They may *extrapolate* beyond what is currently known to develop a plausible continuation of the storyline. Interpolating and extrapolating require students to synthesize context from the details they have discovered to construct a plausible story. Then they imagine the human experience in that story—the successes and failures and emotions. They produce the context from the facts. Creative nonfiction story projects meld imagination creativity skills with information investigation skills to ensure students develop both their convergent and divergent thinking abilities. Combining both creative and analytical thinking results in whole-mind learning.

So how can fact-based imaginative storytelling be combined with the problems-first approach? See the example for a high school history class in figure 10.1.

> The teacher begins the class by explaining to the students that they will be assuming the role of a high school social studies teacher heading into a department meeting, which will be run by the social studies department head. The teacher explains that she will be playing the role of the department head, and the meeting begins.
>
> "I want to pick up on the discussion we were having at the end of the last meeting about how we can help students wrestle with the opposing ideas of working for peace in the world versus needing to take strong action against those who act aggressively to get what they want. Recall that at our last meeting, Mr. Henderson pointed out that that English politicians were wrestling with these two ideas just before the start of World War II.
>
> "To help our students learn this concept, let's create a short play for our students of a fictional conversation between Winston Churchill and Prime Minister Neville Chamberlain, just before Chamberlain left for his meeting with Adolf Hitler in 1939. You will need to pair up, and each partnership must write a play that depicts a plausible interaction between these two historical figures. Make sure that what you write is based upon the actual views that these men held regarding how to deal with Hitler and the Nazis. To help our students understand how you came up with this imaginary conversation, please make a written list of sources for the views held by Chamberlain and Churchill. Include representative quotes from those sources for students to read.
>
> "We want to be able to show this play to all of our social studies classes. Mr. Douglas came up with the idea to make a video showing the plays that each partnership created. That way all students can see the different conversations we have imagined.
>
> "Any questions?"

Figure 10.1: A problem that requires students to engage in creative thinking.

Teach the Entire Writing Process

Is there a way to teach imagination creativity skills in almost all of our classrooms? Is there some aspect of learning that extends across most, if not all, the courses we teach in school? Yes—*writing*.

Teaching students how to write is a major objective for teachers around the world. It has been one of the main goals of education throughout history. Writing and the cognitive process behind it are timeless skills that will remain valid regardless of how the world changes. Teaching students how to write effectively will always be a cornerstone of education.

However, there is significant omission in the way that most students are taught to write. The writing process has five steps: (1) plan, (2) draft, (3) revise, (4) proof, and (5) publish. However, the focus of writing instruction that most students traditionally receive in school is almost solely on the first four steps of this process. Teachers spend a significant amount of effort on the *plan* step of the writing process—teaching students how to do the research to find raw material for their work and how to brainstorm to come up with ideas for their compositions. They give students lots of coaching on organization and logical thought development in the *draft* and *revise* steps of the writing process. They teach spelling and grammar regularly throughout the entire writing process, but they emphasize these aspects in the *proof* step.

For the most part, the goal of the writing process in most courses is for students to demonstrate their understanding of a topic using the convergent thinking skills of analysis and logical deduction. However, the fifth step in the writing process, the *publish* step, is often an afterthought, if it is given any thought at all. For many teachers, publishing consists of printing out a written composition on a white piece of paper.

This process is, for the most part, excellent. Students need to learn how to read analytically to get ideas for their writing. They need to learn how to do effective writing based on logical thought development and how to make points substantiated by their research. They need to learn correct word spelling and the use of proper grammar. These abilities will serve them well for the rest of their lives. However, in the communication age of the 21st century, there are essential presentation skills students need to learn in the *publish* step so that they can present their ideas in ways that go beyond printed words. Teaching students how to use modern multimedia tools when publishing their work will empower them to communicate effectively with modern audiences who are immersed in a multimedia world.

Since the emphasis in writing process instruction is on communicating with written words in reports, essays, lab write-ups, and so on, students naturally assume that doing a good job of crafting the words in a document is all that is needed for effective communication. This is not the case. For example, take the creation of a website.

A student who has been well taught in the first four steps of the writing process may be able to create well-crafted written material, but will not have the ability to create a website that will be truly effective at gaining the attention of people who are surfing the internet. That is because there are other factors in how information is presented that they must address before internet users will engage with written content. The inability to publish written content in a format that meets the expectations of those using the internet results in no communication whatsoever, regardless of a person's writing skill.

In so many arenas, modern information presentation uses visual or audible cues as well as the written word to communicate ideas. We live in a multimedia world. Therefore, we must ensure that every student is equipped with information presentation skills that are relevant in the modern multimedia environment. The publishing step of the writing process is not about the content of a message. Instead, it is about how the students *present* the message to the intended audience.

By fully embracing what it means to publish information in the modern world, we open up our instruction to include teaching students how to use their imaginations to brainstorm creative ways of presenting a message to a target audience, often in an audiovisual format. There are a number of graphical concepts that can be applied to a message to make it come alive and appeal to modern readers. For example, words can become visually appealing items in a design through the clever selection of fonts and the size, position, and color of the text. Color can also be added to a layout through backgrounds, geometric shapes, and images. Applying the graphic design concepts of dominance, balance, contrast, rhythm, and unity to a layout can greatly enhance the communication of a message. These concepts can also be applied to video messages.

Additional concepts apply to shooting video. Storyboarding is an essential step in planning a video. Shooting video using the rule of thirds is an important concept to learn. Lighting can be a particular challenge, and there are a number of skills that must be mastered in order to light a video effectively. Sound recording and choosing the right soundtrack are other important parts of video creation and production, as is learning how to shoot video to communicate a message effectively without using words at all.

Creating a visually appealing presentation to convey a message is another way to bring divergent thinking into the classroom. Generating presentation ideas can occur after students craft a message in the first four steps of the writing process. But it may be necessary to imagine how a message will be presented right at the beginning of the writing process. The medium that will be used to publish a message may have a significant impact on how the writing is done in the first four steps of the writing process. A screenplay for a video, for example, will be written very differently than the content for a website. The important point is that by embracing the complete writing process, we can teach imaginative, divergent thinking skills while we teach the curriculum.

Figure 10.2 (page 94) presents an example of a problems-first project for a high school English class with an enhanced publishing step of the writing process.

> The teacher explains to his class that today the students are going to be assuming the role of members of the creative team for a documentary series for the local public television station. The team will be working on a series of programs on great authors of the 20th century. The creative team has been called to attend a meeting with the series coordinator to discuss the next episode. The teacher informs the class that he will be playing the role of the series coordinator. The teacher begins the role-play by saying the following.
>
> "OK, we need to get going on the remainder of our work on the next installment of the Great Authors series. This month's author is William Golding, and the featured book is *Lord of the Flies*. We have completed our work on the short biography of Golding. Now we need to explore what specifically led him to write *Lord of the Flies*.
>
> "Based on the feedback we received from our viewers on the first three episodes, it is clear that people like the show better when we present an opinion on the author's featured book. So, for our opinion piece, let's focus on the scene in which Simon is speaking with the pig's head, and the Lord of the Flies replies. We want you to state an opinion on who Golding is saying Simon is really talking to in this scene. Then, explain how you think this scene relates to the rest of the book.
>
> "Create a video in documentary format in which you film a narrator who lays out a case in support of your opinion. We want to highlight the brilliance of Golding's writing, so you need to include excerpts from *Lord of the Flies*. You must interpret these excerpts as you build your case. Be sure the visuals in the video for these excerpts support what the narrator is saying. Before you begin filming, please submit the text for the narration in printed form so we can look it over.
>
> "Any questions?"

Figure 10.2: A problem requiring students to consider the publish step of the writing process.

Solving this problem will require students to go through all five steps of the writing process with a focus on the publish step. Now let's explore how to get students to think innovatively.

Enter the Idea-Storm Think Tank

If we want students to develop their innovation creativity skills, we must find a way to break the habit of overemphasizing one-dimensional convergent thinking in our classrooms. We must help students realize there is more than one right answer when solving a problem. We need to get students thinking freely and creatively without worrying about failure if they try something new or different. This is very difficult when so much of the instruction in a school is geared toward preparing students for tests where the focus is on logical, linear, convergent thought that predominantly leads to only one right answer.

If our goal is for students to develop creative, innovative thinking, this means we must get students to start thinking divergently. Divergent thinking is thinking that is free-form and outside the box. Thinking divergently often means breaking the rules. Often, innovative, creative thinking is random thought that dares to go against the status quo, challenges long-standing assumptions, and explores alternatives to the standard way of doing things. While this outside-the-box thinking may seem strange, unproductive, and even reckless, outside-the-box creative, divergent thought is vitally important to all of human progress. Well-known author and leadership expert John C. Maxwell (2003) quotes Charles Kettering, who says, "All human development, no matter what form it takes, must be outside the rules; otherwise we would never have anything new" (p. 115). It is critical that we do our best to foster creative, divergent thinking in our students so they can be active participants in the creative endeavors that contribute to the advancement of human society.

Students must develop their ability to generate new ideas. To help them do so, I recommend setting aside a special time for what I call the *Idea-Storm Think Tank*. This is a time when students are told that the normal rules don't apply. When I tell students, "We are entering the Idea-Storm Think Tank," they know that a whole new set of rules for how to behave is now in effect. I use the Idea-Storm Think Tank during the design step for most projects when introducing students to the problems-first instructional approach. I want students to get in the habit of using the think tank as a vehicle for divergent thinking to produce creative ideas for solving a problem.

The goal is to create a learning environment where the normal expectation for getting right answers does not apply—an environment where we remove students' fear of failure. That is why it is so important to stress that there are special new rules for how to behave in the think tank. Within the Idea-Storm Think Tank, students complete a two-stage process that includes: (1) generate ideas, and (2) apply convergent thinking.

Generate Ideas

Within the first stage of the Idea-Storm Think Tank—generating ideas—we have the following rules.

1. No idea is bad; no idea is wrong.
2. No criticism of someone else's thinking is allowed.
3. Everyone participates.
4. Every idea is recorded, regardless of how silly it may seem.
5. Students work in groups.

These rules are based on sound research on cognitive behavior (Psychology.iresearchnet.com, n.d.; Rothstein & Santana, 2011; Study.com, 2012) and are established to facilitate divergent thinking. (For a more in-depth look at the research behind facilitating divergent thinking, see Rothstein & Santana, 2011.) It takes time for students to become comfortable with the Idea-Storm Think Tank rules, so I start by having students generate ideas for small tasks. In the beginning, I identify an event, a message, a product, or a process I want students to think about. For example, you could use an event like an upcoming election, a terrorist bombing, the signing of a trade treaty, or a local referendum. Products could include a new treatment for cancer, a pesticide, an artificially intelligent robot, a new shopping center, or a self-driving car. Processes could include the water cycle, evaporation, electromagnetism, food distribution, or moving cases through the courts. You can start with things students already know well, such as how something is done in your school, and have students come up with ideas for how it could be improved (for example, improvements regarding the food offered in the school's cafeteria). Or, you can take a topic from course content and have students generate alternative ideas that would produce better results.

The key here is to give a prompt to students to help them start using their imaginations to generate new ideas. Getting students to use their imaginations is important because imagination is needed in every field of endeavor. When I have discussions with science teachers about the skills students need to be successful in science courses, what I hear most often is that students need logical, analytical reasoning skills. Imagination is a word that rarely comes up in these discussions. Yet imagination is at the very heart of scientific work. Albert Einstein himself says, "To raise new questions, new possibilities, to regard old problems from a new angle, requires creative imagination and marks real advance in science" (Einstein & Infeld, 1938, p. 92).

Ideas are essentially *connections*. Your mind figures out a way to connect two or more known things together. Therefore, the first step to take when generating new ideas is to learn everything you can about a particular issue. Once that information is known, you can then begin thinking about how to connect the details in creative ways. This is an ideal time to ask students to apply the synthesis skills of looking for patterns, predicting what comes next, and proposing changes to improve something. There are many tools and techniques that professionals have developed to help people determine the components of a problem and to generate creative connections between them. Some sources for helping students generate ideas include the following.

- "Thinking Methods" (IdeaConnection, n.d.)
- "The Four Most Powerful Types of Creative Thinking" (McGuinness, n.d.)
- "8 Creative Thinking Techniques and the Tools to Use" (Gardiner, 2013)
- "Creative Thinking Techniques" (Brown & Kusiak, 2002)

At first, the Idea-Storm Think Tank can be a special time that is unconnected to other project work that students are doing. It is a fun diversion from the normal activities in a class, and the focus is solely on coming up with lots and lots of ideas. However, once students have become familiar with how the Idea-Storm Think Tank works and have gained some skill in generating creative ideas, it is time to start incorporating the think tank into the four D problem-solving process. The Idea-Storm Think Tank is an excellent way to bring divergent thinking into problem solving because idea generation is a critical part of the design step of the four D problem-solving process.

Apply Convergent Thinking

The second stage of the Idea-Storm Think Tank involves bringing convergent thinking to bear on the ideas that students generated using divergent thinking in the first stage of the idea generation process. To be useful, creativity must *add value* to something. It is not enough to just think creatively; the thinking must lead to something that is constructive or provides some benefit. Students must now apply convergent thinking to their ideas and begin to look at their ideas critically. Will an idea work? Are there factors that mitigate the effectiveness of this idea or render it completely useless? Is this idea cost-effective? Do we have enough time to do this? These are important questions to start asking if we hope to take new thinking from ideas to something applicable in the real world. Asking critical questions also helps students see the relative value of ideas on the list so that they can pick the best idea from all the ideas they have generated.

There are many strategies for choosing the best idea from a list. If the students will be working on a project as a group, a technique that my students have found useful is *sticky voting*. The teacher or a nominated student writes the list of ideas on a whiteboard or a large sheet of paper. Each student then receives some sticky notes (usually three stickies). Then, without discussion, the students place their stickies beside the ideas they think are the best. They can put all their stickies on one idea if they wish. Once everyone is done, it is easy to stand back from the list and see which ideas the students think are the best. This is a great visual technique for arriving at consensus.

Choosing the best idea for solving a problem leads naturally to designing a plan for implementing that creative idea. This is what the design step of the four D problem-solving process is all about—devising a plan to solve a problem. As students gain familiarity and confidence in using the Idea-Storm Think Tank to generate ideas, it quickly becomes an indispensable component of their problem-solving strategy.

Figure 10.3 (page 98) gives an example of a high school problems-first project that can be presented in a number of different courses when the teacher wants to encourage innovative thinking. The problem would work especially well in a business or marketing class. It is ideally suited to using the Idea-Storm Think Tank.

> The teacher begins the class by explaining that today the students are going to take on the role of the vice-principal of their high school. The vice-principal has been called to a meeting at the school district office to discuss how the school distributes learning resources to students. The assistant superintendent and the head of accounting will co-chair the meeting, and the teacher will be playing the role of the assistant superintendent. The meeting begins with the assistant superintendent addressing the group.
>
> "In this meeting, we are going to tackle an important and costly issue for the school district—the distribution of resources to our high school students. We have always used textbooks, but we have two major problems with textbooks that have surfaced in the last few years. First, textbooks are costing the school district an enormous amount of money. Second, a textbook must be in use for several years before we can afford to replace it, but because information in the world today is changing so quickly, the textbooks for science and social studies often contain dated or incorrect information. This is a real problem. So, we need ideas for alternatives to distributing physical textbooks to students. We need a resource to support learning that will provide students with up-to-date information while saving the district money. At this stage, we need you to generate as many ideas as possible.
>
> "Any questions?"

Figure 10.3: A problem that fosters innovative thinking.

Conclusion

There is much talk about the need for teaching creativity skills to prepare students for the modern workplace (Sparks, 2020). Teaching these skills, however, can be a real challenge. The problems-first instructional approach is ideally suited to encourage creative thinking. By incorporating the strategies presented in this chapter, teachers can develop both imagination creativity skills and innovation creativity skills.

The next chapter will focus on assessment of problems-first projects.

QUESTIONS FOR DISCUSSION

Please reflect on the following questions, either on your own or as part of a collaborative teacher team.

1. On which topics can you ask students to use fact-based imagination?
2. How can you implement the full range of modern publishing of written work into the project work you ask your students to do?
3. Create a project in which your students would benefit from using the Idea-Storm Think Tank.

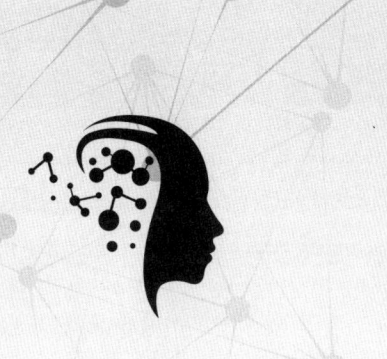

CHAPTER 11
Evaluate Holistically

When thinking about assessment, consider the following questions.

- How well do the assignments and assessments I give measure student learning?
- Do they provide a complete picture of what a student is capable of?
- Am I measuring information recall skill and the ability to follow a series of steps in a procedure, or am I assessing long-term process skill development?
- Can I say with assurance that students understand what the information they have retrieved represents?
- Do students understand the concepts behind the steps they are following?
- Can they make connections in the information they recall?
- Does my instructional approach foster the development of higher-level thinking skills?

These are incredibly important questions that every teacher should ask themselves about instruction and the assessment of learning in their classrooms. Unfortunately, long-standing ways of teaching and assessing can keep people from thinking critically about these important assessment-related issues. I have asserted that the teaching as telling, learning as listening approach to instruction has become entrenched, especially for those who teach in high school and postsecondary institutions. Hand in hand with the teaching as telling, learning as listening approach is a likewise entrenched approach to assessment. Like me, many teachers may have accepted these default approaches without thinking and simply continued to assess their students in the same way they were assessed when they were students themselves.

These default approaches to instruction and assessment are based on the following reasoning (Mueller, 2018b).

1. A major goal of schooling is to train students to become productive people who can contribute to society economically, politically, and socially.
2. A major aspect of being productive is to acquire knowledge and skill in a number of areas, including English, social studies, mathematics, and science.
3. Schools must focus instruction on teaching this knowledge and skill to students.
4. Assessment of learning focuses on gauging how well students have acquired the knowledge and skills that have been taught.

In this approach to instruction, the first step is to determine the body of knowledge and skill that students should learn in a course curriculum. Once the curriculum has been set, educators can create assessments of learning that will gauge how well students have learned the course content. Since the curriculum is developed first, it is said that the *curriculum drives assessment*. This approach to teaching and assessing has been the predominant approach in schools for a long time (Martin, 2017).

The focus on acquiring knowledge has led to teaching with an overemphasis on the skills of low-level information recall and rote memorization of specific procedures. Assessment relies almost solely on test scores as an indicator of student performance. I call this *sponge assessment*—the measure of how much information a student has soaked up while in a course. These widely accepted default approaches to instruction and assessment have not been adequately successful in fostering meaningful learning in students (Ackoff & Greenberg, 2008).

There is, however, another approach to instruction and assessment that looks at learning and assessment from a very different perspective—*authentic assessment*. This chapter will first discuss the concept of authentic assessment and describe several strategies teachers can use within this approach. It will then consider how to utilize formative assessment within the problems-first approach, giving special consideration to the use of rubrics. Finally, it will consider self-assessment as one of the most valuable tools teachers can use in authentic assessment.

Authentic Assessment

In the problems-first teaching approach, tasks have a real-world link that leads students into doing the kinds of tasks they will encounter when they leave the school system. By solving a problem, ownership of learning shifts to the student. The problems-first instructional approach stresses the application of knowledge to complete tasks rather than recall of information. This new way of teaching requires a different way to assess student learning. An authentic approach to teaching calls for an authentic approach to the assessment of student learning.

The following sections will discuss five strategies teachers can use to assess learning in the problems-first approach to instruction.

1. Performance assessment
2. Short analysis
3. Portfolios
4. Peer assessment
5. Student self-assessment

Performance Assessment

Traditional assessment typically measures what a student *knows* about a subject. A performance assessment measures what students can *do* with what they know. Thus, traditional and performance assessment strategies are complementary (Hibbard et al., 1996). A performance assessment determines a student's ability to apply skills to a real-world task. This is the kind of evaluation that is used most often in the world of work. In the workplace, employers don't give multiple choice quizzes to evaluate the quality and effectiveness of their employees' work. Instead, they do performance assessments with their workers to gauge their skill competency when performing the tasks associated with their job. A performance assessment is a demonstration of ability.

The benefits of performance-based assessments in education are well documented. These assessments provide teachers with information about how well a student understands and applies knowledge while providing students with more meaningful and engaging tasks (Brualdi, 2000).

Performance assessment works well with problems-first projects. Figure 11.1 (page 102) presents a performance assessment form with a simplified set of the main assessment criteria for the *Lord of the Flies* (Golding, 1954) video project described in figure 10.2 in the previous chapter (page 94).

Each of these criteria can be expanded for more detailed assessment. Performance assessments are ideally suited to student self-assessment. Notice that the form includes a column for the students to self-assess their performance on the various criteria for the project. Seeing the student's and the teacher's assessments side by side can naturally lead to a discussion of the reasons for the similarity of the evaluations or the gap between them.

Short Analysis

Short analysis can be an excellent way to assess how well students have mastered basic concepts and skills. Short analysis exercises are an excellent strategy for providing

Performance Assessment Form

Student Name:

Project Name:

Measurement Criteria	Possible Marks	Awarded Marks	
		Student	Teacher
1. Define problem with a list of specifications	10		
2. Complete the Solution Design Form	10		
3. Specify intermediate deadlines for subtasks	10		
4. Include analysis of Golding's motivation for writing book	25		
5. Justify opinion of who Simon is really talking to	25		
6. Produce video	25		
7. Use time effectively	15		
8.			
9.			
10.			

Figure 11.1: A performance assessment form with simplified assessment criteria.

Visit go.SolutionTree.com/21stcenturyskills for a free reproducible version of this figure.

formative assessment for learning to students as well as providing valuable feedback to the teacher on how well students are mastering course material. Dylan Wiliam (2006) refers to formative assessment as *assessment for learning*, and short analysis exercises are excellent tools for helping students gauge the progress of their learning. The formative assessment nature of these exercises means that many of them, if not most, do not need to be graded.

Many short analysis exercises use a prompt to enable students to apply what they have learned to a new, short task. The prompt could be a poster, a political cartoon, a mathematics problem, a map, or a short excerpt from an article or book. The teacher may ask students to interpret, describe, calculate, explain, or predict.

Another short analysis exercise is assigning students a one-minute essay on a topic chosen by the teacher. The one-minute writing exercise could also be given near the end of a class period to gauge student learning using prompts like the following.

- What did you learn today, what are you still curious about, and what did you not understand?
- How would you change today's class if you could?
- What was easy to learn today? What was hard?

Visual representation of thinking is another short analysis technique that can be very helpful to gaining insight into what students understand. The teacher asks students to draw a diagram or picture that represents their understanding of a topic. *Concept mapping* is another visual representation of thinking strategy that can be a useful tactic to assess how well students understand relationships among concepts. Students make a visual representation showing the connections between concepts and ideas (see figure 11.2, page 104). Students can sketch a mind map with a pencil and paper or use software tools. There are quite a few pieces of software for creating concept maps, including Mindmaster, FreeMind, Mindomo, and Inspiration, as well as online tools like Sketchboard (https://sketchboard.io/), Coggle (https://coggle.it/), and MindMeister (www.mindmeister.com).

A concept map like the one shown in figure 11.2 (page 104) makes it very easy to see the student's thinking, both in the ideas the student has come up with and in the links between those ideas. Tools like this, which make thinking visible, are invaluable for a teacher because they make the inner thoughts of students easily discernible.

Portfolios

A portfolio is a collection of a student's work. It provides evidence of the learning a student has done over time. Thus, a portfolio provides a much broader view of a student's learning than one can obtain in snapshot assessments like single assignments, quizzes, and tests. This method provides a long-term perspective by documenting a student's improvement and achievements (Study.com, 2016). For the student compiling a collection of his or her work, a portfolio helps the student gain an understanding of the importance of editing his or her work. Scrutinizing their work during the editing process has the added benefit of being a form of self-assessment.

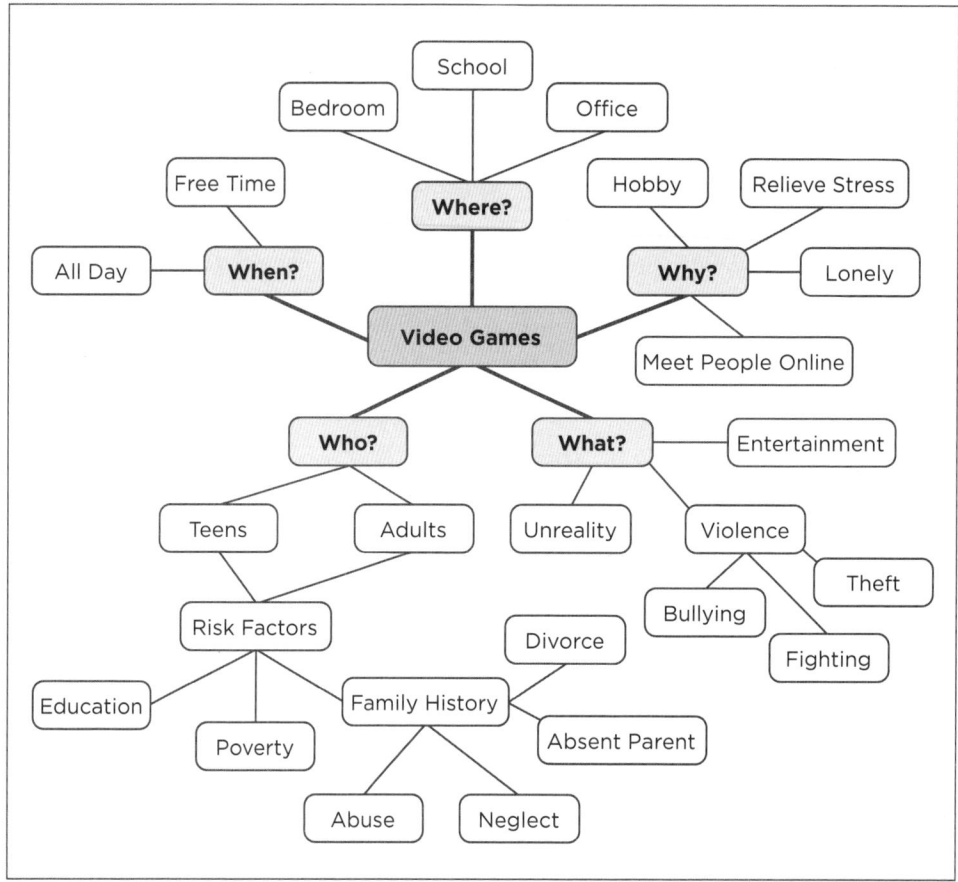

Figure 11.2: A student mind map for ideas stemming from video game use.

There are three main purposes for portfolios (Mueller, 2018a).

1. **Portfolios to demonstrate growth:** These portfolios may contain rough drafts, sketches, and notes from brainstorming sessions as well as completed projects. Students can track the progress of their learning journey by observing how their work has matured over time.
2. **Portfolios to showcase a student's best work:** These portfolios are used for applying for college admission or for employment.
3. **Portfolios to document achievement:** These portfolios are used for summative assessment of student learning for grading purposes.

Growth portfolios provide valuable feedback to students on the progress of their learning. Discussing the rate and nature of the progress with the student can lead to a better picture of strengths and weaknesses. These portfolios need not be graded. Showcase portfolios are for students to showcase or demonstrate their talent to other students, parents, members of the community, or prospective employers. Again, these portfolios are often not graded. Achievement portfolios, however, are used for summative evaluation, and grades are assigned according to how well the work in the portfolio demonstrates that the student has met the objectives for a course.

Peer Assessment

Peer assessment is an excellent way for students to get feedback on their work. It is most helpful when it comes from fellow students who are working on the same task because fellow students have firsthand experience tackling the challenges of the same task. Thus, their feedback can be very insightful and useful for helping the student to make positive adjustments to his or her work.

Peer assessment is a strategy that enables students to receive feedback on their work much more quickly than if they have to wait for feedback from the teacher. Often a teacher does not have the time to give feedback to each individual student. Peer assessment also helps both the student giving the feedback and the student receiving the feedback. The student giving the feedback must examine the project criteria more closely in order to be able to make meaningful comments on the work of another student. This will, of course, help the student receiving the feedback, but it also helps students giving the feedback when they return to their own work (University of British Columbia, n.d.).

Since most students may have had little, if any, experience giving feedback to their fellow students, it is important that the teacher outline clearly what is to be assessed when a student's work is being looked at (Boon, 2020). In addition, the teacher needs to model positive constructive criticism so that students are not unkind when making suggestions to another's work. Students will get better at giving peer assessments with practice. It is best to start with small assessments that only focus on one or two aspects of a project and give students multiple opportunities to practice on these small assessments before increasing the scope of peer assessments. I have found that in the beginning it works best for students to work in pairs so that the one receiving feedback is not overwhelmed with comments from multiple critics.

Self-Assessment

Self-assessment shifts some, if not all, of the responsibility for evaluating work from the teacher to the student. This autonomy has positive benefits for learning. John Wang (2018) indicates that autonomy is one of the three core psychological needs. Students thrive when they are able to make decisions about their learning. Autonomous motivation was found to be associated with numerous positive outcomes, including engagement, creativity, better performance, and persistence at school (Wang, Liu, Kee, & Chian, 2019). Thus, self-assessment has greater positive effects than just the freedom to assess one's own work on a specific project.

Most students see assessment as something that is done to them by someone else and outside their control. Further, often students do not know the criteria for evaluation beyond the letter grade or percentage recorded on their work (Missouri Department of Elementary and Secondary Education, n.d.). Self-assessment aims to address these issues. Because students must assess their own learning, they must become much more aware of the criteria for a project than in traditional assessment to assess how well they have met the objectives for a task. Students can be asked to evaluate the work they have produced, the process they have followed to produce that work, their participation in group activities, and their internal attitude skill development.

There are various strategies teachers can utilize for self-assessment. For example, they can give students a set of criteria and then ask them to self-mark their work. They can ask students questions that require an evaluation of their work, an aspect of the process they are following, or an internal attitude skill. Alternatively, they can also ask students to maintain a journal as a way of keeping track of their self-assessment over time. As students gain experience with self-assessment, teachers can ask them to become involved in the development of the criteria that will be used for the assessment. I have found this strategy of including students in the development of assessment criteria to be effective at fostering student ownership of learning. It encourages student autonomy which, in turn, fosters intrinsic motivation. Researchers Richard M. Ryan and Edward L. Deci (2000) have identified intrinsic motivation as the key factor in an individual reaching his or her potential.

Having students assess their own work lets them take control of their own learning and gives them the chance to manage their own progress and development more independently. Self-assessment increases a student's self-awareness through reflective practice. This helps to develop valuable metacognitive skills that will be very useful in their careers after graduation. Self-assessment also contributes to the development of critical reviewing skills and learning how to evaluate their own performances more objectively (Academ, 2017).

The teacher's role in the self-assessment process is to provide feedback to the student on the validity of the assessment. Teachers may confirm the accuracy of the student's assessment, or they may help the student to understand why the assessment is higher or lower than what the work deserves.

Any of these strategies can be used as a summative assessment, but there is great value in utilizing these methods within formative assessment as well. The following section will discuss the importance of formative assessment and communicating expectations clearly to students through the use of rubrics.

Formative Assessment and Rubrics

In authentic teaching and assessment, a significant shift in emphasis from the traditional focus on summative assessment offers a new focus on the process of learning. New assessment strategies focus on providing meaningful feedback to students while they are learning, to help them make changes before the final assessment for a particular project. Of course, summative assessment of student work must still occur, but the hope is that the feedback from informal formative assessments while students are working on a task will lead to more significant learning and higher-quality final work.

Regardless of the topic, an authentic teaching and assessment approach begins with determining what outcomes you are hoping for when the tasks are complete. With these outcomes decided, you can then choose which authentic assessment technique will be the best at measuring student attainment of those outcomes. Once you have determined the outcomes and methods of assessment, you can work backward to develop the teaching strategies that will be best at guiding your students to those outcomes.

I have found it is critical that students clearly understand the expectations I have for their work. The best tool I have discovered for communicating expectations to students is a rubric. A rubric is an invaluable tool for helping students understand what they must do to perform well on real-world tasks. A rubric is a list of assessment criteria for an attribute of learning. The criteria range from unacceptable to exemplary and are accompanied with descriptions that explain what student work looks like for each level of assessment. The rubric of expectations I give to my students is built upon the goals I have for the project and the standards I am using for evaluating student work.

When using rubrics, you can measure whatever attributes of learning you think are important. One of the great aspects of an authentic teaching and assessment approach is that you can include skills such as internal attitude skills in your assessment, skills that are not typically evaluated during the traditional approach to assessment. It is important to remember the old adage about the need for measuring what you want to see, "What gets measured gets done" (Bredenberg, 2012). If you want students to follow the four D problem-solving process, you must give marks to students for completing each step in the process. If you want students to develop their internal attitude skills, then you give marks for those skills.

It is important to note that the use of authentic assessment versus traditional assessment is not an either-or decision. Traditional assessment tools like quizzes and tests still have a place in ensuring that students commit valuable information to memory. Memorization is not a dirty word—it has an important role to play in learning because you cannot talk intelligently about a topic that you don't know anything about. As Wiggins (2002) states:

> Our line of argument is that testing is a small part of assessment. It needs to be part of the picture. Many people who are anti-testing end up sounding anti-evaluation and anti-measurement. A good test has a role to play. The language that we like to use is, it's an audit. It's a snapshot.

Therefore, traditional assessments are part of a holistic approach to evaluating student learning. However, we must ensure that we do more than just measure knowledge acquisition. We must also use the strategies described here to assess skill development on real-world tasks. See the example projects in chapter 14 (page 129) for rubrics for evaluating skill development.

One vital tool teachers have in their repertoire is self-assessment. The following section will discuss how teachers can utilize this method to improve their assessment practices, especially for attitude skills.

Self-Assessment as a Tool for Assessing Internal Attitude Skills

I want to focus on self-assessment for a moment. Refer to the diagram Progressing to the Highest Levels of Learning in figure 1.2 (page 12), and you will see that a major goal is independence for our students. A significant component of independence is the ability to objectively assess how well one is performing in one's personal and professional life. Teachers must find a way to pass some of the evaluation of a student's schoolwork over to the student in order to give him or her guided practice at personal assessment. Requiring students to look critically at their own work leads to self-reliance and independence. Self-assessment is an essential skill for students because they will be very much on their own when they leave the school system.

Self-assessment also has another value for the teacher—it is an indispensable tool for assessing internal attitude skill development. Often internal attitude skills are just as important to employers as specific job skills. But internal attitude skills are difficult for a teacher to assess because only the student knows what is going on inside his or her head. It is really only the students themselves who can assess the ways in which their attitudes toward their work are improving or deteriorating.

Initially, it may be uncomfortable to have students self-assess their work. Teachers may feel like they are losing control. However, the positive benefits of self-assessment for student learning and for preparing students for life after graduation are compelling. One suggestion is to have a discussion with individual students about their self-assessments to ensure that work is being evaluated appropriately.

Figure 11.3 is an example of how to use a real-world link to encourage students to complete a self-assessment. This problem could take place within almost any junior high school class.

> The teacher begins the class by explaining to the students that they will be taking on the role of engineers at a local engineering firm. They have been working at the company for three months, and it is time for their first performance review. Their supervisor has scheduled a meeting with them to go over what is expected for this performance review. The teacher informs the students that she will be playing the role of their supervisor, and the meeting begins as follows.
>
> "All right, I see it is time for your regular performance review. I also see that this is the first time you have done this, so let me explain why we are doing this and what is expected of you. The main reason we do performance reviews is because when employees are growing personally as well as developing their job skills, the company performs better as well. My goal today is to spend some time with you to help you develop your job skills and your personal productivity skills.
>
> "In your performance review, you will be asked to look back at the last project you completed and assess both the work you produced and the process you followed to produce it. You will be asked to rate yourself in various areas using a number from 1 to 100. Starting with the actual product that you created, rate its overall quality out of 100. Also, provide us with a written evaluation identifying the aspects of the product that were done well and the aspects that could have been done better. Point form is acceptable for the product evaluation write-up.
>
> "Since this is your first performance review, we will be focusing on just three areas for the assessment of the process you followed to create the product— (1) the four Ds, (2) time management, and (3) your attitude. As you know, we ask all our employees to apply the four D problem-solving process when they are doing their work. You will be asked to rate how well you applied each of the four steps in that four D process using a scale of 1 to 100. Also, you will need to provide a written assessment outlining what you did well and what you need to improve upon for each step of the four D process. Please also provide a written assessment of how efficiently you managed your time at each stage of the project.
>
> "You will remember from your new employee orientation meeting that we are striving to create a positive working environment for all of our employees. So, it is very important that you assess your attitude while working on this last project. During the performance review, you will rate how positive your attitude has been out of 100. In addition, you will be required to provide a write-up describing situations in which you have made an effort to be positive as well as situations in which you could have been more positive. For the areas in which you could have been more positive, you will be asked to provide the outline for a strategy that you could use the next time you are faced with a similar situation.
>
> "Your performance review will take place at the end of this week. Please come to the review prepared with all the information that I have requested from you in this meeting.
>
> "Any questions?"

Figure 11.3: Using the problems-first approach to assess internal attitude skills.

Self-assessment is really the only way to evaluate internal attitude skills because only the students really know their attitudes. Using a real-world performance review like this helps students to see the relevance of developing self-evaluation skills. The assessment done by the students in this project provides the teacher with an excellent starting point for a discussion with the students about their progress in developing the kinds of attitude skills that will empower them for success when they leave school.

Conclusion

Evaluating holistically means going beyond the recall of procedures and content to assessing long-term process skill development using more authentic assessment. This chapter outlined five key strategies for authentic assessment that can be implemented with the problems-first instructional approach. It also discussed the benefits of student autonomy.

The next chapter will look at the role the teacher plays in fostering student independence.

QUESTIONS FOR DISCUSSION

Please reflect on the following questions, either on your own or as part of a collaborative teacher team.

1. Evaluating holistically means assessing more about students than just their ability to perform on quizzes and tests and to produce reports. How can you adjust your assessment to assess a student's development of the seven pillar process skills?

2. How can you implement student self-assessment as part of assessment in your courses?

3. How can you implement student portfolios as part of assessment in your courses?

CHAPTER 12

Ease Yourself Out of the Picture

My mother was an amazing woman and a very good parent. When I became a parent myself, I often asked her for tips on parenting. The most significant thing she told me was that as painful as it is to do, it is the job of parents to make themselves obsolete. It was a great insight. Over the course of the first seventeen to twenty years of children's lives, parents equip their children with the skills they need to succeed, and then slowly hand over the reins. They adhere to a fundamental policy of progressively reducing their guidance.

You apply this policy of progressively withdrawing when you teach your children how to walk. When they start learning how to walk, your children need your help—at first, just to stand. Then, as they begin to take their first steps, they are dependent on your assistance to be successful. As they gain ability and confidence, you start withdrawing your help because you want them to stand and walk on their own. And, even though you know they will fall and possibly hurt themselves, you finally let go and let them try it all by themselves. Why do you withdraw? Because you know that they will not learn to walk on their own unless you do. Your child becomes independent because you had the foresight and the courage to withdraw your assistance.

When you think about it, there are many similarities between teaching new things to students in school and teaching young children to walk. Shouldn't student independence be the goal of every teacher—to equip students with the skills they need for success and then progressively withdraw assistance until they can do things on their own?

If we want our students to step confidently out into the real world when they leave school, we must start giving them real-world problems while they are still in school so they can get practice handling the kinds of problems they will be faced with outside the school system. Students need to learn how to deal with information that is progressively less complete. Think about when you made the decision to purchase your first house. Was your decision predetermined for you, or did you have to agonize over all the variables and unknowns? I will bet there were many factors to weigh when making your decision, such as, What are the plans for the vacant property across the street? Is the city going to push through the dead-end road? Does the city have any long-term plans that will change the zoning in this area? What are the neighbors like? How far is it to the closest school? What are interest rates likely to do? Should we lock into a fixed-rate mortgage or let the rate float? When it comes to deciding which house to purchase, you do your research and then you make your best guess based on the incomplete information you have been able to gather. This is the real world and the kind of decision making we need to prepare our students for.

A mistake we sometimes make as teachers is that we don't let go enough. We shouldn't then be surprised when our students graduate and struggle when they encounter the kinds of problems that occur daily in the world outside our classrooms. If we want them to be truly successful in life after school, we start letting go long before they leave us.

What does letting go look like? It looks a lot like the kind of teaching I am proposing in this book. It means embracing a more open-ended approach to instruction that allows students to discover course material on their own. Letting go means embracing the use of student self-assessment not only as an effective way to facilitate learning but also as a way to give students more independence. Letting go also means that a teacher must have a plan for deliberately withdrawing assistance to students so that students can learn to tackle tasks on their own. It does not mean that teachers should not provide any help when students need it, but it does mean that teachers should intervene less and less as students learn to become more and more responsible for their own learning. As this transferring of ownership for learning takes place, our role shifts from being the primary source of instruction to being a learning resource that provides guidance when students ask for our help.

Conclusion

Teachers need to be intentional about giving away the responsibility for learning to their students in order to foster their independence.

The next section of the book (page 115) will focus on practical tips for making the shift to the problems-first instructional approach in your classroom.

QUESTIONS FOR DISCUSSION

Please reflect on the following questions, either on your own or as part of a collaborative teacher team.

1. How do you foster independence in the students you teach?
2. Are you afraid of losing control of the learning if you withdraw from helping students in your classroom? How can you overcome this?
3. How can you plan to progressively withdraw from being responsible for the learning that takes place in the courses you teach?

PART THREE

Making the Shift to Problems-First Teaching

This section provides guidance on how you can make the shift to a problems-first approach. Chapter 13 answers any questions you may have on how to begin using this new approach in classrooms, and chapter 14 provides problems-first projects, including rubrics, to help you plan projects.

CHAPTER 13

Pointers for Shifting to a Problems-First Approach

Much of teaching can become habitual, and it can be just as hard to break out of long-established patterns of teaching behavior as it is to break out of other habitual patterns of behavior. Just think about how difficult it is to change your diet, increase the amount of exercise you do, or break an undesired habit like biting your nails. Changing behavior can be very challenging (DiSalvo, 2017).

Similarly, if you are like me and the invisible force of the long-established teaching as telling, learning as listening approach to instruction has a strong hold on the way you teach, then breaking free of it will require real effort. It is important to remember your motivation for shifting to a new instructional approach: better long-term process skill development that equips students with the tools they will need for lifelong success, while also teaching the curriculum for your course.

This chapter begins by giving readers a list of three things to remember when beginning problems-first teaching. It then presents a process for designing problems-first projects for students in any subject in grades 6 through 12. In combination with the example project plans in the next chapter, this process plan will be invaluable as you begin your journey toward implementing problems-first projects.

Things to Remember When Beginning Problems-First Teaching

Before diving into how to design problems-first projects, there are three important things teachers should remember as they begin adapting their instruction:

1. Employ incremental change at first, with one big change
2. Rely on the four Ds
3. Remember to apply the *poorly principle*

Employ Incremental Change With One Big Change

With incremental change, you begin moving in the general direction of a desired goal, and, through a series of minor adjustments, you gradually head in the direction that will lead to the goal you are aiming at. Movement, no matter how small, is the key. I often tell students who are struggling when contemplating making a change in their lives, "You can't steer a parked car. Just pick a direction and get moving."

Even if it isn't the best direction, because you are moving, you will soon figure out that it's not the right way for you. Then you can steer yourself in a new direction until you get it right. The biggest hindrance to making a successful change is not doing it wrong; it's doing nothing at all. You can't steer if you are standing still.

This also applies to teachers contemplating a change in their teaching practice. Movement, no matter how small, is the key. Start making little changes to the way you do things. In terms of implementing a problems-first approach to instruction, this may mean starting with small projects that take less time than a class period to complete. (See figure 6.2, page 52, for an example of a small problems-first project.) To begin with, you may also choose to do only one problems-first project per month.

However, there is one big change that you must embrace—it is critical to stop telling students what they need to know. You may start out by giving your students a small problems-first project that lasts only a few minutes, but you must stop using telling as your method of instruction. If you are at all like me, then you will have to strongly resist the urge to tell students what to do when they stare back at you in bewilderment the first time you give them a problem to solve on their own. I find that presenting the problem in a role-play is just as helpful for me as it is for the students because, as the role-play character, I do not have the knowledge or skill to solve the problem myself. This helps me to stifle my compulsion to teach by telling.

Rely on the Four Ds

When I was studying computer science in university, I learned about the processes for defining problems and designing successful solutions. I developed the four Ds by distilling the problem-solving process down to the minimum number of steps necessary to create effective solutions. The four Ds (see chapter 7, page 55) are based on solid problem-solving procedure and comprise a problem-solving strategy you can rely on.

Equipping students with the four D problem-solving process gives students an essential tool that will enable them to be successful when they encounter real-world problems that they may not initially know how to solve. By following the four steps of define, design, do, and debrief, students will be able to move forward when encountering challenging tasks that otherwise may have stopped them dead in their tracks. Whenever students are stuck on what to do next, point them back to the four Ds instead of simply telling them what to do. (See figure 7.6, page 68, for a complete diagram of the four Ds. You may like to print this figure out and display it on your classroom wall for easy reference.)

Apply the Poorly Principle

The *poorly principle* states that anything worth doing is worth doing poorly at the start (while you learn how to do it well). This is a great principle to pass on to anyone learning any new skill, especially if learning that skill is proving to be challenging. Any good coach or teacher understands the poorly principle and knows their athletes or students will do poorly when they begin learning something new. The coach or teacher gets his or her athletes or students to work on the new skill over and over again to gain proficiency. The only way to progress in skill development is to practice.

Likewise, planning and teaching problems-first projects requires skill. Therefore, the poorly principle means that teachers cannot expect to have instant success when they start using the problems-first approach to instruction. Understand that it will require practice to gain proficiency at planning and teaching with this method of instruction. You must resist the urge to abandon the approach because it does not go perfectly at the beginning.

A Process for Designing Problems-First Projects

To help you understand the procedure for designing a problems-first project, figure 13.1 (page 120) contains a flowchart to follow. This flowchart identifies important questions to ask, either on your own or as part of a teacher team, as you create problems for your students. We will consider each part of the flowchart in the following sections.

Be Double-Minded

Any project we ask students to do starts with the curriculum for the course we are teaching. So, like any other lesson, you begin by identifying the course content you need to cover. However, be of two minds when you are planning a problems-first project by also considering how the work you are requiring of students can be used to teach the long-term seven pillar process skills.

Curricular Goals

There are curriculum guides to follow for all courses in middle school and high school, so this is the logical place to start when planning a new project. Consider the standards your state's curriculum requires, in addition to any subject-specific goals.

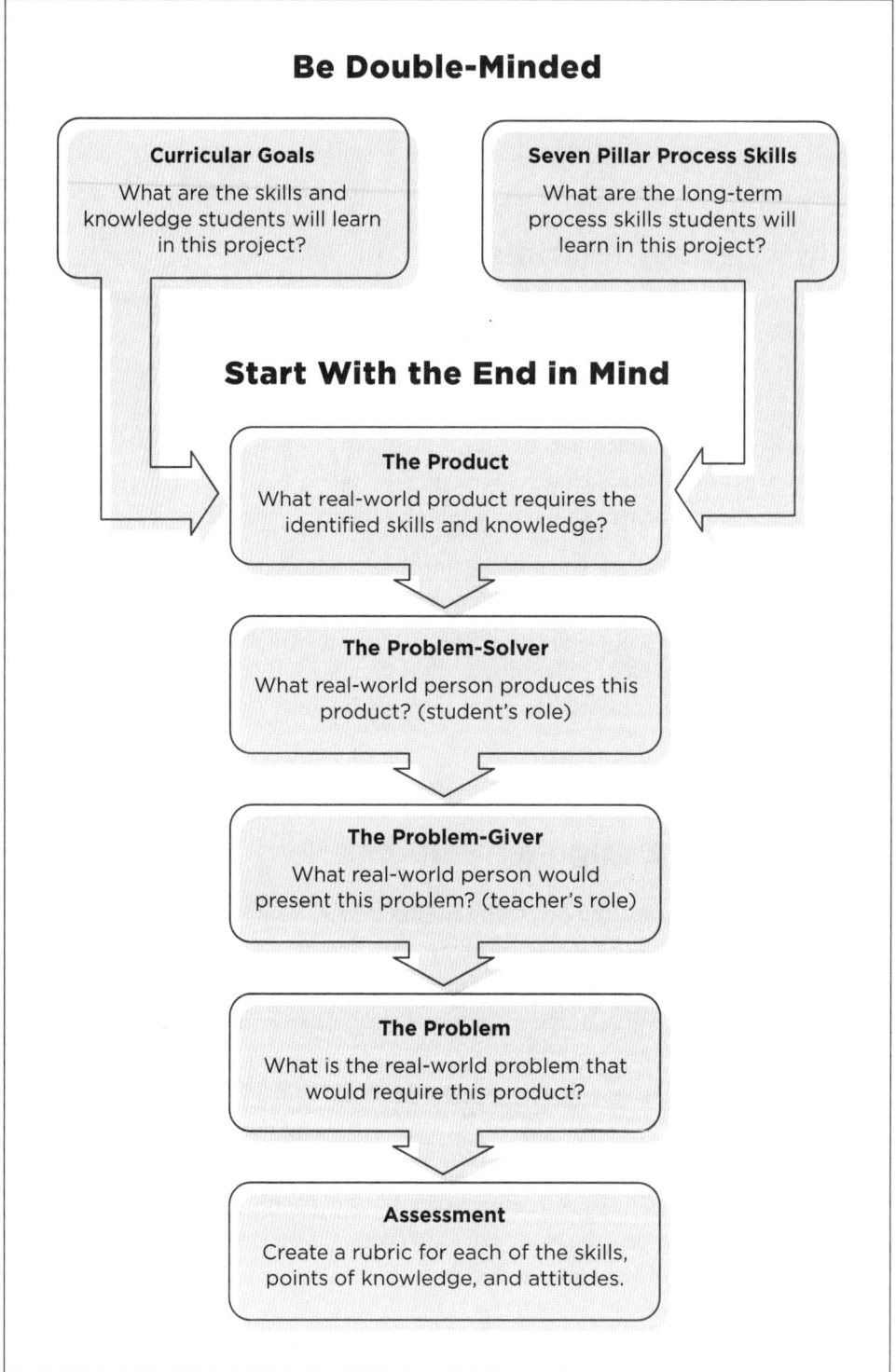

Figure 13.1: The problems-first project planning flowchart.

Visit go.SolutionTree.com/21stcenturyskills for a free reproducible version of this figure.

Once you have established these curricular goals, it's time to consider the curriculum as an instrument for also teaching students valuable process skills.

Seven Pillar Process Skills

These long-term process skills may or may not be listed in the curriculum guide for your course, but that doesn't mean they should be overlooked. I would argue that long-term process skills are the most important skills we teach our students because they are the skills they will use over and over again for the rest of their lives. You may decide not to address all seven pillars in a project. Choose which of the seven pillar process skills you want students to develop in this particular project.

The Product

At this stage, consider the end of the project. In problems-first learning, producing a product is the main way for students to demonstrate what they have learned. The product is the focus of the project for the students, and the attributes you specify for the product will lead students into the desired learning. This is an important point. You must think backward by first establishing the specifications for a product that will require students to use the skills you target to create that product.

As I have discussed, a key to planning problems-first projects is to have a real-world link to the work you have students do. Here is where you may have to do some research about the kinds of things people do in various jobs outside the school system and the kinds of products they produce. Students respond positively when they can clearly see that what they are being asked to produce is a real product that can be found in the world outside school.

The following list contains some examples of products students might produce.

- Magazine article
- Rebuilt small engine
- Sculpture
- Editorial for a newspaper
- Poster
- Survey of public opinion on a particular topic
- Menu plan for a family
- Political speech
- Website
- Scientific experiment
- Memo to someone else in a business or organization
- Wiring diagram for a new house
- Short story
- Screenplay for a movie
- Advertisement in a print publication
- Mash-up of songs
- Geotechnical analysis of a building site
- Script for an original play
- Design for a new building

- Advertisement for TV
- Drawing
- Documentary video
- Design for a new layout for a part of a city
- Original song
- Piece of furniture
- Presentation to local city council, state or provincial government, or other stakeholder
- Painting
- Fully built garden shed

The specifications for the product are a critical component of the project. These specs will lead students into the knowledge and skills you have set as your goals. For example, if you have the goal of having students develop their information investigation skills in a video project where the students take on the role of television news journalists, you might specify that the topic is a video story showing two sides of the illegal drug problem—those who favor decriminalizing illegal drugs and those who don't. Further, you might specify that to spark a debate on the subject, the television station wants the journalist to end the story by taking a position on the issue.

The Problem-Solver

Identify an occupation for the student to role-play for this project. Ask yourself, "Who in the real world would produce the product I selected in the previous step?" This is another area where you may want to do some research on the kinds of tasks people do in various occupations outside the school system. The student's role can be anyone in the world outside school.

The following list contains examples of roles that students might assume.

- Plumber
- Chef
- Scientific engineer
- Farmer
- Environmentalist with a YouTube channel
- Journalist
- Legal researcher
- Metal fabricator
- Speechwriter
- Physiotherapist
- High school principal
- Nurse
- Appliance repairman
- Photographer
- Electronics technician
- Hair stylist
- Advisor to a politician
- Psychiatrist
- Dietitian
- Computer programmer
- Airline pilot
- Political blogger
- Pharmacist
- Car mechanic
- Fashion designer

- Laboratory technician
- Actor
- Graphic artist
- Electrician
- Playwright
- TV news camera person
- Travel agent

The Problem-Giver

Identify the role-play character the teacher will assume for this project. Ask yourself, "Who in the real world would request this kind of product from the role-play character the students are assuming?"

The following are some examples of the role-play character the teacher could assume as the problem-giver.

- Boss or supervisor in a business or organization
- Concerned citizen
- Family member
- Client of a business
- Politician
- Public servant
- Homeowner
- Physician
- Judge
- Government official
- Police officer
- Patient in the emergency room of a hospital
- Librarian
- Military officer
- Pet owner
- Newspaper editor

The Problem

Devise a problem that would require the production of the desired product, and then write a script for how the problem-giver will present this problem to the problem-solver. The key to outlining the problem to your students without telling them how to go about solving it is for the teacher to role-play the person who has the job you identified for the problem-giver. In character, the teacher will not be able to answer students' questions about how to solve the problem because the problem-giver is seeking the problem-solver's help precisely because he or she does not know how to solve the problem that is being presented.

Write a scenario for how the problem-giver will present the problem to the problem-solvers. Scenarios for the problem can be very modest when you begin to implement the problems-first instructional approach (see figure 13.2, page 124, for an example).

However, problems should become more complex as you and your students gain familiarity with this method of instruction and learning.

> The teacher begins the class by saying:
>
> "Today you are going to be working as reporters for the local newspaper. You have just been called to an emergency meeting with the chief editor for the paper. I will be assuming the role of the chief editor."
>
> The chief editor begins the meeting as follows.
>
> "The reporter responsible for the literature review section of the newspaper has been called away on an urgent personal matter. She didn't get all her writing done before she left. That means we need you to write a two hundred word literature review article. As you know, the mid-week edition of the paper goes to press in just one hour, so we need this article fast. Read this poem titled, "The Road Not Taken," by Robert Frost, and write your opinion on what you think the author is saying. Remember, I need this article finished and delivered to me in one hour.
>
> "Any questions?"

Figure 13.2: An example of a modest problems-first project.

In order to more fully develop your students' problem definition skills, when presenting the problem as the problem-giver, consider withholding pertinent information. The students will be required to more fully define the problem by asking questions that probe more deeply into the nature of the task they are required to do.

Assessment

Create a rubric for each of the attributes you want to measure during and at the end of the project. There are different strategies for creating the criteria for a rubric. A four-point scale is helpful to assess how well a student is performing on a particular attribute of learning. The scale generally has the following four criteria for assessing a student's proficiency on learning attributes.

1	2	3	4
Not meeting expectations	Minimally meeting expectations	Fully meeting expectations	Exceeding expectations

The new British Columbia curriculum (British Columbia Ministry of Education, n.d.a) follows this general pattern.

You can give assessment rubrics to students ahead of time so they know how you intend to grade a project. This will help students self-assess their work. In addition, these rubrics are excellent tools for providing students with formative assessments as they are working their way through a problem.

The book *Introduction to Rubrics: An Assessment Tool to Save Grading Time, Convey Effective Feedback, and Promote Student Learning* by Dannelle D. Stevens and Antonia

J. Levi (2013) is an excellent resource for more fully exploring the use of rubrics in assessment.

The Goal of Complex Problem Solving

Referring to the list of top ten skills people will need for success that was presented at the beginning of chapter 2 (page 15), I must note that it's not just problem solving we need to teach our students—it's the ability to independently solve *complex* problems. The problems-first approach allows teachers to progress toward complex problem solving in their courses.

There are three important components in making this happen. First, we must equip our students with the four D problem-solving process. This process is an invaluable tool that students can apply over and over again throughout their entire lives. Second, we must increase the complexity of the problems that we give our students to solve. Increasing the complexity of problems means increasing the number of interrelated factors that are contributing to the reasons for a problem. When students are first learning how to problem solve, we give them simple problems to tackle that have only one or two factors to consider. These problems are not like the multifaceted problems that people encounter in the world outside school, but we need to start with very controlled situations that have limited causes so we do not overwhelm our students. But as students progress in their problem-solving ability, we need to increase the complexity of the problems they must solve by introducing more factors for them to consider when they are designing a solution. This way, we can better prepare students for the kinds of problems they will face in the world outside school.

Third, we must progressively withdraw the amount of help we give to students as they advance in their ability to apply the four D problem-solving process. This does not mean we stop helping students altogether, but it does mean we increasingly step back from intervening and volunteering assistance when students encounter difficulties. We want students to move toward independence in their problem-solving ability.

Figure 13.3 (page 126) illustrates how the responsibility for solving problems changes over time.

It may seem counterintuitive that we withdraw the amount of support we give our students, but we must remember that our goal is to get our students to think independently. If we equip students with problem-solving process skills, then we will empower them to tackle difficult and complex problems without any help from us.

As you and your students gain familiarity with the problems-first approach, it will be time for you to develop a plan for increasing the complexity of the problems students must tackle over the duration of a course of study. The key is to ensure that students

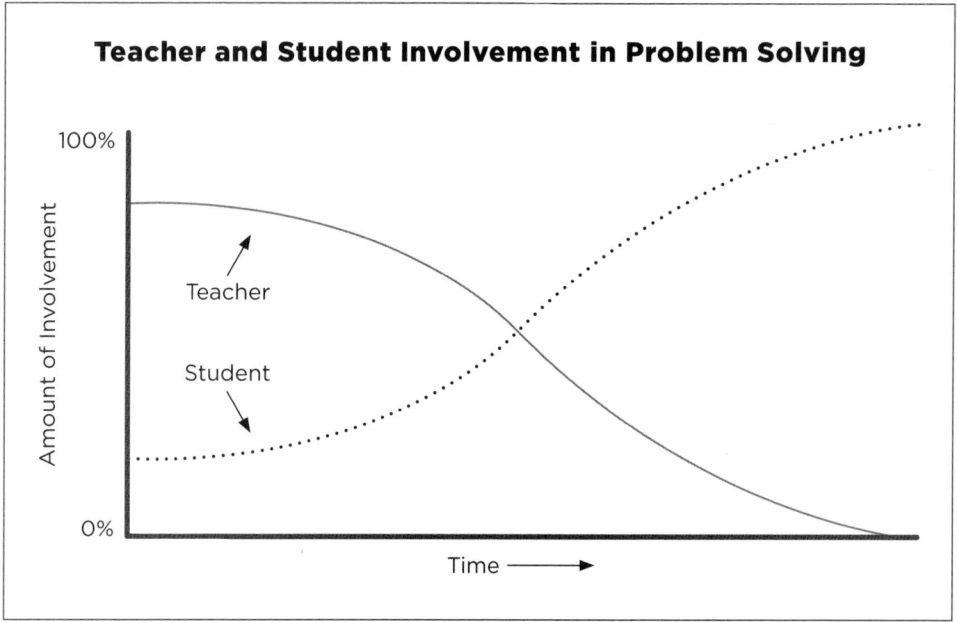

Figure 13.3: How the responsibility for problem solving changes over time.

have sufficient practice in applying the four Ds to a variety of simple problems before they face significantly more difficult tasks. If possible, two or more teachers, or even entire departments, could get together to create a plan for increasing the complexity of problems that spans two or more courses.

One Project Per Term

It might seem overwhelming to think about doing a number of these types of projects in your classes every term. If you acknowledge the validity of this method of teaching by making the shift to giving students a series of problems-first projects, but it seems like it will require too much time and effort, I have a proposal for you to consider—do just one problems-first project with your students next term.

Consider the impact on the learning experience for students if every middle school and high school teacher gave just one problems-first project to their students each term. Just one project per teacher would have a significant positive effect on student learning. Student engagement would increase. Most importantly, students would be better prepared to solve the problems they will face when they leave the school system.

Conclusion

This chapter has presented several tips for shifting to the problems-first instructional approach. Following these suggestions should make it possible for any teacher to incorporate problems-first projects into their teaching.

The next chapter will provide examples of complete problems-first projects to further help you understand the development of these tasks for students.

QUESTIONS FOR DISCUSSION

Please reflect on the following questions, either on your own or as part of a collaborative teacher team.

1. When was the last time you did poorly or failed completely at doing something new in the way you teach (not what you teach, but the way you teach)? Did that poor performance or outright failure cause you to abandon that new practice? Why or why not?

2. How could you use the problems-first project planning flowchart (see figure 13.1, page 120) to implement the problems-first approach in the classes you teach?

3. What single problems-first project could you give to your students next term in a course you teach?

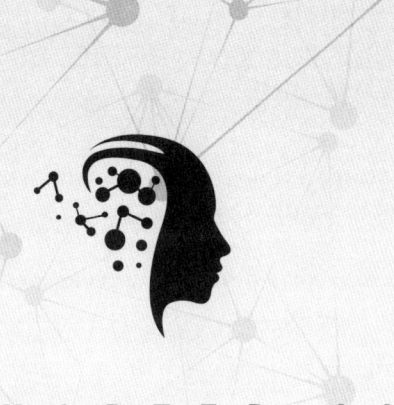

CHAPTER 14

Examples of Problems-First Lesson Plans

To help you as you begin implementing problems-first projects in your classroom, I am including three examples of problems-first project plans to guide you. This chapter will present examples of problems-first projects for (1) a junior high science class (page 129), (2) a middle school English language arts class (page 134), and (3) a junior high social studies class (page 138).

An Example of a Problems-First Project Plan for a Junior High School Science Class

Here is an example that follows the steps outlined in the problems-first project planning flowchart (figure 13.1, page 120) to design a project for a junior high school science class.

Curricular Goals

The project aims to address the following curricular goals.

- Student can explain how each of the following elements behaves when exposed to a flame—oxygen, hydrogen, and carbon monoxide.

- Student can explain the procedure of using a flame to determine whether a colorless, odorless gas is oxygen, hydrogen, or carbon monoxide.

- Student can explain the safety procedures necessary when exposing a colorless, odorless gas such as oxygen, hydrogen, or carbon monoxide to a flame.

129

Seven Pillar Process Skill Goals

The project aims to address the following seven pillar process skills. (Additional seven pillar process skill goals can be added to subsequent assignments once students have had more experience doing problems-first projects.)

- Student can determine what must be done to solve a problem during the define step of the four Ds.
- Student, when doing the design step of the four Ds, can identify the knowledge and expertise he or she needs to acquire to tackle the assigned problem.
- Student will develop information investigation skills by finding information relevant to a specific problem.
- Student will develop imagination creativity skills by using a video camera and video editing software to create an instructional video with video effects to enhance communication.
- Student will assess how well the video explains the procedure for safely doing this experiment during the debrief step of the four Ds.
- Student will assess the quality of the video during the debrief step of the four Ds.

The Product

This project aims to create a short instructional video explaining the procedure for using a flame to determine whether a colorless, odorless gas is oxygen, hydrogen, or carbon monoxide. The video must also explain and demonstrate the safety procedures for doing this procedure in a chemistry lab.

The Problem-Solver

The student will assume the role of a lab technician working in a chemistry lab for an oil company.

The Problem-Giver

The teacher will assume the role of the maintenance supervisor working at a remote oil drilling facility.

The Problem

The teacher will explain to the students that they will be taking on the role of chemical lab technicians at a research facility for an oil company. They are about to get a phone call from the maintenance manager of the company's drilling operation outside

Nome, Alaska. The teacher informs the students that the teacher will be playing the role of the maintenance manager.

The teacher begins the role-play by saying:

> *"Hello, it's Rob Jones, the maintenance manager at the Nome Operation in Alaska calling. We have a real problem here, and we need some help. One of the maintenance workers accidentally punctured a pipe, and we now have a gas leak. The gas is odorless and colorless. Using the blueprints for the pipes in the facility, we have been able to narrow the identity of the gas down to oxygen, hydrogen, or carbon monoxide. The problem is that we don't know exactly which type of gas is leaking and whether or not the gas is dangerous. All of the chemical technicians have left for a three-week break, so we are all alone here. We have access to the chemistry lab, but none of us are really trained in how to figure out what kind of gas is leaking. We don't know what to do next. We are concerned that we may not have fixed all of the leaks, and since it is possible that we may create a spark when we are doing the rest of the maintenance work, we are worried about causing an explosion. We need to know whether or not it's safe for us to continue working. This leak is a serious concern for us, so we need your help right away.*
>
> *"We have captured some of the gas in a 10 mL container. What we need from you is a video showing us how to determine which of the three possible gases is in that container and what will happen if the gas is exposed to a spark or flame. Please begin your video by showing us how to set up the lab so that we can do this procedure safely—we don't want to blow ourselves up! Please email the video by the end of the week.*
>
> *"Any questions?"*

Since the problem is presented verbally, students will need to listen carefully, take good notes, and ask appropriate questions in order to define the problem accurately and understand clearly what they are being asked to do. I have found when students initially encounter a problems-first project, they often want to ask me questions about the problem after the role-play problem-giver (Mr. Jones) has left. I respond by telling the students that I don't know the answers to their questions—they need to ask Mr. Jones. If this is the first time they have been given a problems-first project, Mr. Jones may need to make a return visit. However, in subsequent projects, students soon learn that they need to pay close attention the first time around because Mr. Jones will not be coming back.

Assessment

Figure 14.1 (page 132) presents the rubric for assessing the students' learning in this project. You can share this rubric with students before they begin work on the project so they can self-assess their learning as they are working.

- Student can explain how each of the following elements behaves when exposed to a flame—oxygen, hydrogen, and carbon monoxide.

1	2	3	4
Student cannot explain how any of the elements behave when exposed to a flame	Student can minimally explain how the elements behave when exposed to a flame	Student can adequately explain how the elements behave when exposed to a flame	Student can fully explain how the elements behave when exposed to a flame

- Student can explain the procedure of using a flame to determine whether a colorless, odorless gas is oxygen, hydrogen, or carbon monoxide.

1	2	3	4
Student cannot explain the procedure	Student can explain some of the procedure	Student can explain most of the procedure	Student can explain the complete procedure

- Student can explain the safety procedures necessary when exposing a colorless, odorless gas such as oxygen, hydrogen, or carbon monoxide to a flame.

1	2	3	4
Student cannot explain the safety procedure	Student has minimally identified the elements of the safety procedure	Student has identified most of the elements of the safety procedure	Student has identified all of the elements of the safety procedure

- Student can determine what must be done to solve a problem during the define step of the four Ds. Specifically, for this project:
    - learn the procedure for determining whether the 10 mL container is holding oxygen, hydrogen, or carbon monoxide
    - learn the safety procedures for doing the experiment safely
    - create a video that demonstrates how to safely do this experiment

1	2	3	4
Student has not listed most of the criteria for the project	Student has listed some of the criteria for the project	Student has listed most of the criteria for the project	Student has listed all of the criteria for the project

- Student, when doing the design step of the four Ds, can identify the knowledge and expertise he or she needs to acquire to tackle the assigned problem.

1	2	3	4
Student has not identified any of the knowledge or expertise needed for the project	Student has identified some of the knowledge and expertise needed for the project	Student has identified most of the knowledge and expertise needed for the project	Student has identified all of the knowledge and expertise needed for the project

- Student will develop information investigation skills by finding information relevant to a specific problem.

1	2	3	4
Student has not found any relevant information to complete the project	Student has found some relevant information to complete the project	Student has found all relevant information to complete the project	Student has found more information than is required to complete the project

- Student will develop imagination creativity skills by using a video camera and video editing software to create an instructional video with video effects to enhance communication.

1	2	3	4
Student has not created an instructional video	Student has created a video that uses unedited footage	Student has created a video that employs transitions, sound effects, and music	Student has created a video that employs transitions, sound effects, music, and video effects

- Student will assess how well the video explains the procedure for safely doing this experiment during the debrief step of the four Ds.

1	2	3	4
Student has not assessed the quality of their video	Student has minimally assessed the quality of their video	Student has adequately assessed the quality of their video	Student assessment of the quality of their video is exceptional

- Student will assess the quality of the video during the debrief step of the four Ds.

1	2	3	4
Student has not assessed the quality of their video	Student has minimally assessed the quality of their video	Student has adequately assessed the quality of their video	Student assessment of the quality of their video is exceptional

Figure 14.1: An example problems-first project for a junior high school science class.

An Example of a Problems-First Project Plan for a Middle School English Language Arts Class

Here is an example that follows the steps outlined in the problems-first project planning flowchart (figure 13.1, page 120) to design a project for a middle school English language arts class.

Curricular Goals

The project aims to address the following curricular goals.

- Student can explain three strategies for effective note-taking.
- Student can identify main themes when taking notes.
- Student can link points to main themes when taking notes.

Seven Pillar Process Skill Goals

The project aims to address the following seven pillar process skills. (As students gain experience doing problems-first projects, additional seven pillar process skill goals can be added to subsequent assignments.)

- Student can determine what must be done to solve a problem during the define step of the four Ds.
- Student, when doing the design step of the four Ds, can ask probing questions of the problem-giver to get needed information about the problem.
- Student, when doing the design step of the four Ds, can identify the knowledge and expertise he or she needs to acquire to tackle the assigned problem.
- Student will develop information investigation skills by finding information relevant to a specific problem.
- Student will develop information investigation skills by making a recommendation based on the information he or she has found.
- Student will develop imagination creativity skills by using a video camera and video editing software to create a video presentation with video effects to enhance communication.
- Student will assess how well the video explains three note-taking strategies during the debrief step of the four Ds.
- Student will assess the quality of the video during the debrief step of the four Ds.

The Product

Students will produce a video presentation on effective note-taking strategies.

The Problem-Solver

Students will assume the role of a marketing manager who has just been recently hired by a financial investment firm—the BRW Investing Company.

The Problem-Giver

The teacher will assume the role of president of the BRW Investing Company.

The Problem

The teacher explains to the students that they will be taking on the role of a newly hired marketing manager for the BRW Investing Company. The marketing manager is responsible not only for promoting the company's investment services to prospective clients but also for all internal communication within the company. The marketing manager is about to receive a visit from the company's president to discuss a problem concerning internal communication in the firm. The teacher informs the students that the teacher will be assuming the role of the company president.

The teacher begins the role-play by saying:

> *"Since you are new to the company, I want to explain a key part of our business. The effectiveness of the financial planning and investing services that we provide to our clients is dependent on projected lending rates and what will be happening in the economy in the near future. To get the most up-to-date information on where things are headed in the economy, several times a year, we send company representatives to presentations given by bankers, economists, and government representatives. We expect our representatives to return with a comprehensive set of notes on what each expert said and to distribute those notes to all employees in the company. This way, BRW can give the most up-to-date and best possible financial and investing advice to our clients.*
>
> *"The problem is that the representatives we are sending to the presentations are not bringing back notes that adequately describe enough of the content the experts presented. As marketing manager, internal communication is your responsibility, so we want you to take the lead on handling this problem. We need you to create an instructional video on effective note-taking strategies. The biggest issue the note-takers have is identifying the main themes of a presentation and relating the details of the presentation to those main themes. We would like the video you create to cover at least three strategies for capturing those main themes, and we want you to make a recommendation as to which note-taking strategy you think is best. We would like to put the video on the company's server in two weeks' time.*
>
> *"Any questions?"*

Assessment

Figure 14.2 (page 136) presents the rubric for assessing the students' learning in this project. You can share this rubric with students before they begin work on the project so they can self-assess their learning as they are working.

- Student can explain three strategies for effective note-taking.

1	2	3	4
Student has not explained any strategies for effective note-taking	Student has explained one strategy for effective note-taking	Student has explained two strategies for effective note-taking	Student has explained three strategies for effective note-taking

- Student can identify main themes when taking notes.

1	2	3	4
Student has not described any strategies for identifying main themes	Student has minimally described how to identify main themes	Student has fully described how to identify main themes	Student has described more than one way to identify main themes

- Student can link points to main themes when taking notes.

1	2	3	4
Student has not described any strategies for linking points to main themes	Student has minimally described how to link points to main themes	Student has fully described how to link points to main themes	Student has described more than one way to link points to main themes

- Student can determine what must be done to solve a problem during the define step of the four Ds. Specifically, for this project:
    - learn at least three note-taking strategies
    - recommend which note-taking strategy is best
    - create a video that teaches the note-taking strategies

1	2	3	4
Student has not listed most of the criteria for the project	Student has listed some of the criteria for the project	Student has listed most of the criteria for the project	Student has listed all of the criteria for the project

- Student, when doing the design step of the four Ds, can ask probing questions of the problem-giver to get needed information about the problem.

1	2	3	4
Student has not asked any questions of the problem-giver	Student has asked basic questions of the problem-giver	Student has asked deeper questions of the problem-giver	Student has asked questions that fully probe the problem-giver for deep answers

- Student, when doing the design step of the four Ds, can identify the knowledge and expertise he or she needs to acquire to tackle the assigned problem.

1	2	3	4
Student has not identified any of the knowledge or expertise needed for the project	Student has identified some of the knowledge and expertise needed for the project	Student has identified most of the knowledge and expertise needed for the project	Student has identified all of the knowledge and expertise needed for the project

- Student will develop information investigation skills by finding information relevant to a specific problem.

1	2	3	4
Student has not found any relevant information to complete the project	Student has found some relevant information to complete the project	Student has found all the relevant information to complete the project	Student has found more information than is required to complete the project

- Student will develop information investigation skills by making a recommendation based on the information he or she has found.

1	2	3	4
Student has not made a recommendation for the best strategy for note-taking	Student has minimally described the reasons for their recommendation for the best strategy for note-taking	Student has adequately described the reasons for their recommendation for the best strategy for note-taking	Student description of the reasons for their recommendation for the best strategy for note-taking is exceptional

- Student will develop imagination creativity skills by using a video camera and video editing software to create a video presentation with video effects to enhance communication.

1	2	3	4
Student has not completed an instructional video	Student has created a video that uses unedited footage	Student has created a video that employs transitions, sound effects, and music	Student has created a video that employs transitions, sound effects, music, and video effects

Figure 14.2: An example problems-first project for a middle school language arts class.

continued →

- Student will assess how well the video explains three note-taking strategies during the debrief step of the four Ds.

1	2	3	4
Student has not assessed the quality of their explanation	Student has minimally assessed the quality of their explanation	Student has adequately assessed the quality of their explanation	Student assessment of the quality of their explanation is exceptional

- Student will assess the quality of the video during the debrief step of the four Ds.

1	2	3	4
Student has not assessed the quality of their video	Student has minimally assessed the quality of their video	Student has adequately assessed the quality of their video	Student assessment of the quality of their video is exceptional

An Example of a Problems-First Project Plan for a Junior High School Social Studies Class

Here is an example that follows the steps outlined in the problems-first project planning flowchart (figure 13.1, page 120) to design a project for a junior high school social studies class.

Curricular Goals

The project aims to address the following curricular goals.

- Student must be able to explain the geography of coastal Lebanon.
- Student must be able to explain the current politics in Lebanon.
- Student must be able to explain the transportation infrastructure of Lebanon.

Seven Pillar Process Skill Goals

The project aims to address the following seven pillar process skills. (As students gain experience doing problems-first projects, additional seven pillar process skill goals can be added to the assignment.)

- Student can determine what must be done to solve a problem during the define step of the four Ds.

- Student, when doing the design step of the four Ds, can ask probing questions of the problem-giver to get needed information about the problem.
- Student, when doing the design step of the four Ds, can identify the knowledge and expertise he or she needs to acquire to tackle the assigned problem.
- Student will develop information investigation skills by finding information relevant to a specific problem.
- Student will develop information investigation skills by taking relevant screenshots of roads in coastal Lebanon in Google Maps.
- Student will develop information investigation skills by making a recommendation based on the information he or she has found.
- Student will develop imagination creativity skills by creating a presentation using slideshow software like PowerPoint or Keynote.
- Student will develop interdependent collaboration skills by developing a plan for dividing the project work between two people.
- Student will develop interdependent collaboration skills by setting intermediate deadlines for subtasks in the project.
- Student will assess how well the presentation explains the suitability of coastal Lebanon for the e-bike tour during the debrief step of the four Ds.
- Student will be able to identify the aspects of the project that were done well during the debrief step of the four Ds.
- Student will assess the quality of the presentation during the debrief step of the four Ds.
- Student will be able to identify the aspects of the project that need improvement during the debrief step of the four Ds.
- Student will assess their time management during the debrief step of the four Ds.

The Product

The student will produce a presentation for the board of directors of the World-Wide Cycling Tours Company on the suitability of coastal Lebanon for a new five-day cycling tour using slideshow software like PowerPoint or Keynote.

The Problem-Solver

The student will assume the role of tour planner for the World-Wide Cycling Tours Company.

The Problem-Giver

The teacher will assume the role of president of the World-Wide Cycling Tours Company.

The Problem

The teacher explains to the students that they will be assuming the role of tour planners for the World-Wide Cycling Tours Company. The tour coordinator is being called to the boss's office (the president of the company) for a meeting. The teacher informs the students that the teacher will be assuming the role of the president.

The teacher begins the role-play by saying:

"Thank you for coming. I want to outline a new project for you. About ten years ago, our company stopped doing tours in the Middle East due to the political instability and violence in that region. We did this reluctantly because there is some wonderful terrain for cycling in those countries, and our clients really enjoyed the tours we offered there. Our board of directors thinks it is time to take another look at that area of the world, and we want to consider Lebanon as the site for possibly doing a five-day tour on our new e-bikes. More specifically, we have chosen the coast of Lebanon as the first place to consider for a tour next summer.

"What we need from you is a report on the suitability of coastal Lebanon for the tour based on the following factors.

- *The safety of our clients in Lebanon considering the political stability and likelihood of violence.*
- *Transportation options for clients to get from the Beirut Airport to the Lebanon coast.*
- *The suitability of the road infrastructure for cycling.*

"We also want you to recommend a possible route for the five-day tour. As I mentioned, clients will be using the new e-bikes that have a maximum range of fifty miles. To make sure the bikes do not run out of power, we want you to find a route for the tour that has daily destinations that are no more than forty miles apart.

"You will need to make a presentation to the board at next month's board meeting. Any relevant visuals you can find of the area will be very helpful, especially those that support your suggestions for the tour. We would definitely like to see screen captures from Street View in Google Maps to show the actual road conditions for possible cycling routes. The presentation must contain your recommendation for whether or not we should move forward with plans to offer a tour in coastal Lebanon. Please make sure to state the reasons for why you have made this recommendation. We recognize that this is a lot to ask in such a short time, so we want you to work with another tour planner as a partner on this project.

"Any questions?"

Assessment

Figure 14.3 presents the rubric for assessing the students' learning in this project. You can share this rubric with students before they begin work on the project so they can self-assess their learning as they are working.

- Student must be able to explain the geography of coastal Lebanon.

1	2	3	4
Student has not explained any of the geography of coastal Lebanon	Student has minimally explained some of the geography of coastal Lebanon	Student has adequately explained the geography of coastal Lebanon	Student has fully explained the geography of coastal Lebanon

- Student must be able to explain the current politics in Lebanon.

1	2	3	4
Student has not explained any of the current politics of Lebanon	Student has minimally explained some of the current politics of Lebanon	Student has adequately explained the current politics of Lebanon	Student has fully explained the current politics of Lebanon

- Student must be able to explain the transportation infrastructure of Lebanon.

1	2	3	4
Student has not explained any of the transportation infrastructure	Student has minimally explained the transportation infrastructure	Student has adequately explained the transportation infrastructure	Student has fully explained the transportation infrastructure

- Student can determine what must be done to solve a problem during the define step of the four Ds. Specifically, for this project:
    - learn about the political stability in Lebanon
    - learn the transportation options for getting from the Beirut Airport to coastal Lebanon
    - take screenshots of the roads in coastal Lebanon using Street View in Google Maps
    - assess the suitability of the roads in coastal Lebanon for an e-bike tour
    - determine the location of a five-day e-bike tour with overnight stops that are no more than forty miles apart
    - make a recommendation for whether or not to go ahead with this e-bike tour
    - create a presentation for the board of directors that outlines the results of this investigation
    - include images to illustrate what is being described

1	2	3	4
Student has not listed most of the criteria for the project	Student has listed some of the criteria for the project	Student has listed most of the criteria for the project	Student has listed all of the criteria for the project

Figure 14.3: An example problems-first project for a junior high school social studies class.

continued →

- Student, when doing the design step of the four Ds, can ask probing questions of the problem-giver to get needed information about the problem.

1	2	3	4
Student has not asked any questions of the problem-giver	Student has asked basic questions of the problem-giver	Student has asked deeper questions of the problem-giver	Student has asked questions that fully probe the problem-giver for deep answers

- Student, when doing the design step of the four Ds, can identify the knowledge and expertise he or she needs to acquire to tackle the assigned problem.

1	2	3	4
Student has not identified any of the knowledge or expertise needed for the project	Student has identified some of the knowledge and expertise needed for the project	Student has identified most of the knowledge and expertise needed for the project	Student has identified all the knowledge and expertise needed for the project

- Student will develop information investigation skills by finding information relevant to a specific problem.

1	2	3	4
Student has not found any relevant information to complete the project	Student has found some relevant information to complete the project	Student has found all relevant information needed to complete the project	Student has found more information than is required to complete the project

- Student will develop information investigation skills by taking relevant screenshots of roads in coastal Lebanon in Google Maps.

1	2	3	4
Student has not found any relevant screenshots of roads in coastal Lebanon	Student has found some relevant screenshots of roads in coastal Lebanon	Student has found an acceptable number of screenshots of roads in coastal Lebanon	Student has found more screenshots of roads in coastal Lebanon than were required

- Student will develop information investigation skills by making a recommendation based on the information he or she has found.

1	2	3	4
Student has not described the reasons for their recommendation for whether to go ahead with this bike tour	Student has minimally described the reasons for their recommendation for whether to go ahead with this bike tour	Student has adequately described the reasons for their recommendation for whether to go ahead with this bike tour	Student fully describes the reasons for their recommendation for whether to go ahead with this bike tour

- Student will develop imagination creativity skills by creating a presentation using slideshow software like PowerPoint or Keynote.

1	2	3	4
Student has not completed a slideshow presentation	Student has created a basic slideshow presentation	Student has created a presentation that uses transitions, sound effects, and music	Student has created a presentation that uses transitions, sound effects, music, and text animations

- Student will develop interdependent collaboration skills by developing a plan for dividing the project work between two people.

1	2	3	4
Student has not developed a plan to divide the project work	Student has developed a partial plan to divide the project work	Student has developed an unbalanced plan with one partner doing more work	Student has developed a balanced plan that divides the work equally

- Student will develop interdependent collaboration skills by setting intermediate deadlines for subtasks in the project.

1	2	3	4
Student has not set any intermediate deadlines for project subtasks	Student has set some intermediate deadlines for project subtasks	Student has set most intermediate deadlines for project subtasks	Student has set all intermediate deadlines for project subtasks

- Student will assess how well the presentation explains the suitability of coastal Lebanon for the e-bike tour during the debrief step of the four Ds.

1	2	3	4
Student has not assessed the quality of their explanation	Student has minimally assessed the quality of their explanation	Student has adequately assessed the quality of their explanation	Student assessment of the quality of their explanation is exceptional

- Student will be able to identify the aspects of the project that were done well during the debrief step of the four Ds.

1	2	3	4
Student has not identified any aspects of the project that were done well	Student has identified some of the aspects of the project that were done well	Student has identified most of the aspects of the project that were done well	Student has identified all of the aspects of the project that were done well

- Student will assess the quality of the presentation during the debrief step of the four Ds.

1	2	3	4
Student has not assessed the quality of their presentation	Student has minimally assessed the quality of their presentation	Student has adequately assessed the quality of their presentation	Student assessment of the quality of their presentation is exceptional

- Student will be able to identify the aspects of the project that need improvement during the debrief step of the four Ds.

1	2	3	4
Student has not identified any aspects of the project that need improvement	Student has identified some of the aspects of the project that need improvement	Student has identified most of the aspects of the project that need improvement	Student has identified all of the aspects of the project that need improvement

- Student will assess their time management during the debrief step of the four Ds.

1	2	3	4
Student has not met any intermediate deadlines for completing project subtasks	Student has met some intermediate deadlines for completing project subtasks	Student has met most intermediate deadlines for completing project subtasks	Student has met all intermediate deadlines for completing project subtasks

Conclusion

Teaching as telling, learning as listening is deeply ingrained in the school system, especially as students progress to higher grade levels. Unfortunately, this approach is not the most effective way to instruct. The goal of this book is to present you with an alternative way to teach your students—the problems-first approach. Starting your instruction of subject material by presenting it as a problem to be solved has many benefits. It naturally engages students in the learning required to come up with a solution. It encourages students to take part in three-dimensional higher-level thinking. It shifts the responsibility for learning to the students. Problems-first learning also enables the teacher to cover the content in the curriculum guide while *at the same time* teaching students the valuable process skills that they will need for long-term success in the world outside school.

The examples of problems in this chapter outline the development of complete problems-first projects, including assessment rubrics. When you consider these examples, along with the other examples of problems-first projects throughout the book, it is my hope that you will see that the problems-first approach to instruction can be used in a wide range of courses at various grade levels. The challenge before you now is to apply the problems-first approach to a course that you teach. Remember that you don't have to use this approach on every project. Start with one problems-first project per term. Also, start with small projects, and expect some trials and tribulations as you gain experience with this new way of teaching. The end result will be rich and relevant learning for your students.

QUESTIONS FOR DISCUSSION

Please reflect on the following questions, either on your own or as part of a collaborative teacher team.

1. What projects that you currently give to your students can you convert to the problems-first format?
2. How can you incorporate teaching the seven pillars of success process skills into your projects?
3. What strategy or strategies can you use to make your assessment more authentic?

REFERENCES AND RESOURCES

Academ. (2017, April 4). *The importance of student self-assessment.* Accessed at https://academ.com.au/importance-student-self-assessment/ on September 4, 2020.

Ackoff, R. L., & Greenberg, D. (2008). *Turning learning right side up: Putting education back on track.* Upper Saddle River, NJ: Prentice Hall.

Anderson, L. W., & Krathwohl, D. R. (Eds.). (2001). *A taxonomy for learning, teaching, and assessing: A revision of Bloom's taxonomy of educational objectives.* New York: Longman.

Barker, E. (2017). *Wondering what happened to your class valedictorian? Not much, research shows.* Accessed at https://money.com/valedictorian-success-research-barking-up-wrong/ on August 7, 2020.

Blenko, M. W., Mankins, M., & Rogers, P. (2010). *The decision-driven organization.* Accessed at https://hbr.org/2010/06/the-decision-driven-organization on August 9, 2020.

Bloom, B. S. (Ed.). (1956). *Taxonomy of educational objectives: The classification of educational goals; Handbook I: Cognitive domain.* New York: David McKay.

Boon, S. (2020). *Using peer assessment as an effective learning strategy in the classroom.* Accessed at https://impact.chartered.college/article/using-peer-assessment-effective-learning-strategy-classroom/ on September 4, 2020.

Bredenberg, A. (2012, December 2). *Who said, "What gets measured gets managed"?* [Blog post]. Accessed at athinkingperson.com/2012/12/02/who-said-what-gets-measured-gets-managed on October 23, 2019.

British Columbia Ministry of Education. (2019, July). *Social studies K-10—Curricular competencies.* Accessed at https://curriculum.gov.bc.ca/sites/curriculum.gov.bc.ca/files/curriculum/continuous-views/en_social_studies_k-10_curricular_competencies.pdf on August 10, 2020.

British Columbia Ministry of Education. (n.d.a). *A framework for classroom assessment.* Accessed at curriculum.gov.bc.ca/sites/curriculum.gov.bc.ca/files/pdf/assessment/a-framework-for-classroom-assessment.pdf on September 21, 2019.

British Columbia Ministry of Education. (n.d.b). *BC's redesigned curriculum: An orientation guide.* Accessed at curriculum.gov.bc.ca/sites/curriculum.gov.bc.ca/files/Curriculum_Brochure.pdf on June 12, 2019.

British Columbia Ministry of Education. (n.d.c). *Thinking.* Accessed at https://curriculum.gov.bc.ca/competencies/thinking on August 12, 2020.

Brown, D., & Kusiak, J. (2002). *Creative thinking techniques.* Accessed at www.miun.se/siteassets/fakulteter/nmt/summer-university/creativethinkingpdf on September 12, 2019.

Brualdi, A. (2000). *Implementing performance assessment in the classroom.* Accessed at www.ascd.org/publications/classroom-leadership/feb2000/Implementing-Performance-Assessment-in-the-Classroom.aspx on September 4, 2020.

Buck Institute for Education. (n.d.). *What is PBL?* Accessed at www.pblworks.org/what-is-pbl on August 4, 2020.

Butler, D. (2016). *Tomorrow's world.* Accessed at www.nature.com/news/polopoly_fs/1.19431!/menu/main/topColumns/topLeftColumn/pdf/530398a.pdf?origin=ppub on August 1, 2020.

Chowdhry, A. (2018). *Artificial intelligence to create 58 million new jobs by 2022, says report.* Accessed at www.forbes.com/sites/amitchowdhry/2018/09/18/artificial-intelligence-to-create-58-million-new-jobs-by-2022-says-report/#7fd6f6c34d4b on August 8, 2020.

Copp, T. (2019). *Juno Beach: Day of courage.* Accessed at www.thecanadianencyclopedia.ca/en/article/juno-beach-feature on July 11, 2019.

Dale, E. (1984). *The educator's quotebook.* Bloomington, IN: Phi Delta Kappa Educational Foundation.

Darling-Hammond, L. (1997). *The right to learn: A blueprint for creating schools that work.* San Francisco: Jossey-Bass.

Daub, T. (2014, May 12). *University lectures are ineffective for learning, analysis finds.* Accessed at www.pbs.org/newshour/science/university-lectures-ineffective-learning-analysis-finds on July 31, 2020.

Dewey, J. (1990). *The school and society; and, The child and the curriculum.* Chicago: University of Chicago Press.

DiSalvo, D. (2017). *8 reasons why it's so hard to really change your behavior.* Accessed at www.psychologytoday.com/ca/blog/neuronarrative/201707/8-reasons-why-its-so-hard-really-change-your-behavior on September 7, 2020.

Drez, R. J. (n.d.). *Juno Beach: World War II.* Accessed at www.britannica.com/place/Juno-Beach on May 4, 2018.

Duke, N. K., & Halvorsen, A. (2017). *New study shows the impact of PBL on student achievement.* Accessed at www.edutopia.org/article/new-study-shows-impact-pbl-student-achievement-nell-duke-anne-lise-halvorsen on August 4, 2020.

Editors of Encyclopaedia Britannica. (n.d.). *Are there really right-brained and left-brained people?* Accessed at www.britannica.com/story/are-there-really-right-brained-and-left-brained-people on March 8, 2019.

Einstein, A., & Infeld, L. (1938). *The evolution of physics.* Cambridge, England: Cambridge University Press.

Fensel, D., & Motta, E. (2001). Structured development of problem solving methods. *IEEE Transactions on Knowledge and Data Engineering, 13*(6), 913–932. Accessed at https://pdfs.semanticscholar.org/c095/282137b63d823f27fea2c43e880b31c82fda.pdf on April 16, 2020.

Filev, A. (2019). *Agile vs. top-down management: Leadership must evolve as an organization matures.* Accessed at www.forbes.com/sites/andrewfilev/2019/03/26/agile-vs-top-down-management-leadership-must-evolve-as-an-organization-matures/#1cd735c35941 on August 9, 2020.

Free Management eBooks. (n.d.). *The six step problem solving model.* Accessed at www.free-management-ebooks.com/news/six-step-problem-solving-model on May 11, 2019.

Frost, R. (2017). *Selected poems of Robert Frost.* New York: Sterling.

Gardiner, H. (2013). *8 creative thinking techniques and the tools to use.* Accessed at www.koozai.com/blog/content-marketing-seo/eight-awesome-creative-thinking-techniques-plus-tools on September 12, 2019.

Glasser, W. (1998). *The quality school teacher: A companion volume to the quality school.* New York: Harper Perennial.

Golding, W. (1954). *Lord of the flies.* London: Faber and Faber.

Gray, A. (2017). *Goodbye, maths and English. Hello, teamwork and communication?* Accessed at www.weforum.org/agenda/2017/02/employers-are-going-soft-the-skills-companies-are-looking-for/ on August 1, 2020.

Hathaway, J. C. (n.d.). *Why yesterday's skills aren't enough to survive today's digital transformation.* Accessed at https://trainingindustry.com/magazine/issue/why-yesterdays-skills-arent-enough-to-survive-todays-digital-transformation/ on August 1, 2020.

Hattie, J., & Clarke, S. (2019). *Visible learning: Feedback.* New York: Routledge.

Heitin, L. (2014). *Finding overlap in the common math, language arts, and science standards.* Accessed at https://ed.stanford.edu/in-the-media/finding-overlap-common-math-language-arts-and-science-standards on November 13, 2020.

Henderson, R. (2015). *What gets measured gets done. Or does it?* Accessed at www.forbes.com/sites/ellevate/2015/06/08/what-gets-measured-gets-done-or-does-it/#34b257aa13c8 on October 23, 2019.

Hendry, E. R. (2013). *7 epic fails brought to you by the genius mind of Thomas Edison.* Accessed at www.smithsonianmag.com/innovation/7-epic-fails-brought-to-you-by-the-genius-mind-of-thomas-edison-180947786 on August 21, 2019.

Henley, B. (2015). *Is creative thinking genetic or learned? We might all be wrong.* Accessed at www.skyword.com/contentstandard/is-creative-thinking-genetic-or-learned-we-might-all-be-wrong/ on August 4, 2020.

Hennessy, B. (2015). *I wish Drucker never said it.* Accessed at billhennessy.com/simple-strategies/2015/09/09/i-wish-drucker-never-said-it on October 23, 2019.

Hibbard, K. M., Van Wagenen, L., Lewbel, S., Waterbury-Wyatt, S., Shaw, S., Pelletier, K., et al. (1996). *Chapter 1. What is performance-based learning and assessment, and why is it important?* Accessed at www.ascd.org/publications/books/196021/chapters/What_is_Performance-Based_Learning_and_Assessment,_and_Why_is_it_Important¢.aspx on September 2, 2020.

IdeaConnection. (n.d.). *Thinking methods.* Accessed at www.ideaconnection.com/thinking-methods on September 12, 2019.

Jarrett, C. (2012, June 27). *Why the left-brain right-brain myth will probably never die* [Blog post]. Accessed at www.psychologytoday.com/ca/blog/brain-myths/201206/why-the-left-brain-right-brain-myth-will-probably-never-die on October 15, 2018.

Johnson, B. (2019). *4 ways to develop creativity in students.* Accessed at www.edutopia.org/article/4-ways-develop-creativity-students on August 4, 2020.

Jonassen, D. H. (2000). Toward a design theory of problem solving. *Educational Technology Research and Development, 48*(4), 63–85. Accessed at link.springer.com/article/10.1007/BF02300500 on March 23, 2019.

Jukes, I., McCain, T., & Crockett, L. (2010). *Understanding the digital generation: Teaching and learning in the new digital landscape.* Thousand Oaks, CA: Corwin Press.

Juno Beach. (n.d.). In *Wikipedia.* Accessed at en.wikipedia.org/wiki/Juno_Beach on May 5, 2018.

King, K. (2018). *Wanted: Employees who can shake hands, make small talk.* Accessed at www.wsj.com/articles/wanted-experts-at-soft-skills-1544360400 on August 8, 2020.

Kingston, S. (2018). *Project based learning & student achievement: What does the research tell us?* Accessed at https://files.eric.ed.gov/fulltext/ED590832.pdf on August 4, 2020.

Kirton, J., & Barham, L. (2005). Information literacy in the workplace. *The Australian Library Journal, 54*(4), 365–376.

Lombrozo, T. (2013, December 2). *The truth about the left brain / right brain relationship.* Accessed at www.npr.org/sections/13.7/2013/12/02/248089436/the-truth-about-the-left-brain-right-brain-relationship on September 1, 2020.

Luenendonk, M. (2019, September 19). *Idea generation: Divergent vs. convergent thinking.* Accessed at www.cleverism.com/idea-generation-divergent-vs-convergent-thinking/ on August 1, 2020.

Martin, J. (2017, June 22). *Science of learning: Assessment driven curriculum.* Accessed at www.linkedin.com/pulse/science-learning-assessment-driven-curriculum-jesse-martin on September 2, 2020.

Maslow, A. (1954). *Motivation and personality.* New York: Harper.

Maxwell, J. C. (2003). *Thinking for a change: 11 ways highly successful people approach life and work.* New York: Hachette.

McConnell, B. (2019, November 28). *What is brainstorming? And why is it important?* Accessed at https://blog.mindmanager.com/blog/2019/11/what-is-brainstorming-and-why-is-it-important/ on August 4, 2020.

McGuinness, M. (n.d.). *Lesson 5: The four most powerful types of creative thinking.* Accessed at lateralaction.com/creative-thinking on September 12, 2019.

McNeece, A. (2020). *Loving what they learn.* Bloomington, IN: Solution Tree Press.

Miller, A. (2015). *When grading harms student learning.* Accessed at www.edutopia.org/blog/when-grading-harms-student-learning-andrew-miller on August 4, 2020.

Missouri Department of Elementary and Secondary Education. (n.d.). *Guidance for using student portfolios in educator evaluation.* Accessed at https://dese.mo.gov/sites/default/files/Portfolio-Handbook.pdf on September 3, 2020.

Montessori, M. (1912). *The Montessori method: Scientific pedagogy as applied to child education in "the children's houses" with additions and revisions by the author* (A. E. George, Trans.). New York: Frederick A. Stokes. (Original work published 1909)

Mueller, J. (2018a). *Portfolios.* Accessed at http://jfmueller.faculty.noctrl.edu/toolbox/portfolios.htm on September 4, 2020.

Mueller, J. (2018b). *What is authentic assessment?* Accessed at http://jfmueller.faculty.noctrl.edu/toolbox/whatisit.htm on September 12, 2019.

Osth, A. (2019, October 28). *Giving your memories physical or emotional context may help you remember them better.* Accessed at www.businessinsider.com/giving-memories-context-helps-you-remember-better-2019-10 on August 4, 2020.

Phillpott, S. (2019). *The importance of interpersonal skills in the workplace.* Accessed at www.careeraddict.com/the-importance-of-interpersonal-skills-in-the-workplace on August 7, 2020.

Piaget, J. (1970). *Science of education and the psychology of the child* (D. Coltman, Trans.). New York: Orion Press.

Pietrangelo, A. (2019, March 7). *Left brain vs. right brain: What does this mean for me?* Accessed at www.healthline.com/health/left-brain-vs-right-brain#left-brainright-brain-theory on September 1, 2020.

Pink, D. H. (2006). *A whole new mind: Why right-brainers will rule the future.* New York: Penguin Group.

Planbox. (2019, January 29). *Idea management: What it is and why it is important for your business.* Accessed at www.planbox.com/idea-management-what-it-is-and-why-it-is-important-for-your-business/ on August 4, 2020.

Psychology.iresearchnet.com. (n.d.). *Brainstorming.* Accessed at http://psychology.iresearchnet.com/social-psychology/group/brainstorming/ on September 2, 2020.

Quast, L. (2011). *Workers of the future will need different skills than in the past. Are you ready?* Accessed at www.forbes.com/sites/lisaquast/2011/12/12/workers-of-the-future-will-need-different-skills-than-in-the-past-are-you-ready/#2e80d2a41e03 on August 1, 2020.

Quotes.net. (n.d.). *Albert Einstein quotes.* Accessed at www.quotes.net/quote/62883 on September 5, 2019.

Randstad. (n.d.). *Want to be sought after by employers? Learn this skill.* Accessed at www.randstad.ca/job-seeker/career-resources/career-development/want-to-be-sought-after-by-employers-learn-this-skill/ on August 9, 2020.

Reeves, D., & Reeves, B. (2017). *The myth of the muse: Supporting virtues that inspire creativity.* Bloomington, IN: Solution Tree Press.

Rothstein, D., & Santana, L. (2011). *Make just one change: Teach students to ask their own questions.* Cambridge, MA: Harvard Education Press.

Ryan, R. M., & Deci, E. L. (2000). *Self-determination theory and the facilitation of intrinsic motivation, social development, and well-being.* Accessed at https://selfdeterminationtheory.org/SDT/documents/2000_RyanDeci_SDT.pdf on September 5, 2020.

Saba. (n.d.). *Why are employee self-evaluations so important?* Accessed at www.saba.com/resources/how-tos/why-are-employee-self-evaluations-so-important on August 4, 2020.

Sayre, E. (2013). *Integrating student-centered learning to promote critical thinking in high school social studies classrooms.* Accessed at https://pdfs.semanticscholar.org/9b11/7440781a1ae62f9a3855bd11b1cb7feb27bb.pdf on August 12, 2020.

Siegesmund, A. (2017, May 11). *Using self-assessment to develop metacognition and self-regulated learners.* Accessed at https://academic.oup.com/femsle/article/364/11/fnx096/3814095 on August 31, 2020.

Simon, H. A., & Newell, A. (1958). Heuristic problem solving: The next advance in operations research. *Operations Research, 6*(1), 1–10.

Sparks, S. D. (2020, February 4). *A creativity conundrum: Can schools teach students to innovate?* Accessed at www.edweek.org/ew/articles/2020/02/05/a-creativity-conundrum-can-schools-teach-students.html on September 2, 2020.

Stevens, D. D., & Levi, A. J. (2013). *Introduction to rubrics: An assessment tool to save grading time, convey effective feedback, and promote student learning* (2nd ed.). Sterling, VA: Stylus.

Stone, E. (2017, September 6). *The science behind the growing importance of collaboration.* Accessed at https://insight.kellogg.northwestern.edu/article/the-science-behind-the-growing-importance-of-collaboration on August 9, 2020.

Strauss, V. (2017, July 11). *It puts kids to sleep—but teachers keep lecturing anyway. Here's what to do about it.* Accessed at www.washingtonpost.com/news/answer-sheet/wp/2017/07/11/it-puts-kids-to-sleep-but-teachers-keep-lecturing-anyway-heres-what-to-do-about-it/ on August 1, 2020.

Study.com. (2012, August 6). *Cognitive thinking: Creativity, brainstorming and convergent & divergent thinking.* Accessed at https://study.com/academy/lesson/cognitive-thinking-creativity-brainstorming-and-convergent-divergent-thinking.html on August 8, 2020.

Study.com. (2016, July 14). *What is a student portfolio? - Ideas & examples.* Accessed at https://study.com/academy/lesson/what-is-a-student-portfolio-ideas-examples.html on September 4, 2020.

Sulla, N. (2012). *Teaching the digital generation.* Accessed at www.educationworld.com/a_curr/teaching-digital-generation.shtml on August 1, 2020.

Tarvin, A. (n.d.). *The 5 steps of problem solving.* Accessed at www.humorthatworks.com/learning/5-steps-of-problem-solving on May 11, 2019.

Team MyHub. (2020). *Collaboration skills: Does your team have what it takes 2020?* Accessed at www.myhubintranet.com/collaboration-skills/ on August 9, 2020.

University of British Columbia. (n.d.). *Ideas and strategies for peer assessments.* Accessed at https://isit.arts.ubc.ca/ideas-and-strategies-for-peer-assessments/ on September 4, 2020.

University of Iowa. (n.d.). *8-step problem solving process.* Accessed at hr.uiowa.edu/development/organizational-development/lean/8-step-problem-solving-process on May 11, 2019.

Vygotsky, L. S. (1978). *Mind in society: The development of higher psychological processes.* Cambridge, MA: Harvard University Press.

Wang, J. (2018). *The joy of learning: What it is and how to achieve it.* Accessed at https://merl.nie.edu.sg/documents/JoyofLearning.pdf on September 5, 2020.

Wang, J., Liu, W. C., Kee, Y. H., & Chian, L. K. (2019). *Competence, autonomy, and relatedness in the classroom: Understanding students' motivational processes using the self-determination theory.* Accessed at www.sciencedirect.com/science/article/pii/S240584401935604X#! on September 5, 2020.

Webb, J. (Executive producer). (1951–1959). *Dragnet* [TV series]. Los Angeles: Mark VII.

Wiggins, G. P. (1993). *Assessing student performance: Exploring the purpose and limits of testing.* San Francisco: Jossey-Bass.

Wiggins, G. P. (2002). *Defining assessment.* Accessed at www.edutopia.org/grant-wiggins-assessment on October 3, 2018.

Wiggins, G., & McTighe, J. (2005). *Understanding by design* (2nd ed.). Alexandria, VA: Association for Supervision and Curriculum Development.

Wiliam, D. (2006). *Assessment for learning: Why, what and how.* Accessed at https://www.google.com/url?sa=t&rct=j&q=&esrc=s&source=web&cd=&ved=2ahUKEwiY4rXtt9DrAhWDJTQIHeT-AmQQFjAKegQIFRAB&url=https%3A%2F%2Fdylanwiliam.org%2FDylan_Wiliams_website%2FPapers_files%2FCambridge%2520AfL%2520keynote.doc&usg=AOvVaw3Sbrq7dJsLFYlyc5bKBFnU on September 4, 2020.

Wittman, J. (n.d.). *The forgetting curve.* Accessed at www.csustan.edu/sites/default/files/groups/Writing%20Program/forgetting_curve.pdf on July 31, 2020.

Wolpert-Gawron, H. (2015). *What the heck is project-based learning?* Accessed at www.edutopia.org/blog/what-heck-project-based-learning-heather-wolpert-gawron on August 4, 2020.

World Economic Forum. (2016). *The future of jobs.* Accessed at www.weforum.org/reports/the-future-of-jobs on July 17, 2019.

Wowbix Marketing. (2019). *Importance of graphic design: 7 reasons with examples.* Accessed at wowbixmarketing.com/importance-of-graphic-design/ on August 4, 2020.

Wurman, R. S. (1989). *Information anxiety.* New York: Doubleday.

Zaentz, S. (Producer), & Forman, M. (Director). (1984). *Amadeus* [Motion picture]. United States: The Saul Zaentz Company.

INDEX

A

Amadeus (Shaffer), 90
analysis/analyzing
    short analysis assessments, 101–103
    steps for, 80–82
Anderson, L., 78, 79
Apple, Inc., 22
ask-probe-evaluate process, 21
assessments
    about, 99–100
    authentic teaching and, 32–34
    conclusion, 110
    example for English language arts class, 135–138
    example for science class, 131–133
    example for social studies class, 140–144
    formative assessments and rubrics, 107–108
    information analysis and, 81
    information investigation skills and, 21
    internal attitude skills and, 108–110
    problems-first projects and, 124–125
    questions for discussion, 110
    types of/authentic assessments, 100–106
autonomy
    fostering autonomy, 111–112
    self-assessment and, 105, 108–110

B

Bloom's taxonomy, 78–79

C

change, 118
Clarke, S., 20
collaboration skills, interdependent, 19, 25–26
communication skills
    imagination creativity skills and, 22
    interdependent collaboration skills and, 26
    interpersonal skills and, 24–25
    role-playing and, 49, 50
complex problem-solving, 26, 125–126
concept mapping, 103, 104
content traps, 77
convergent thinking
    creative nonfiction and, 91
    educating the whole mind and, 89
    Idea-Storm Think Tank and, 95, 97
    independent problem-solving skills and, 27
    information investigation skills and, 21
    information synthesis and, 82
    three-dimensional thinking and, 17–18
    writing process and, 92
creative nonfiction, 90
creativity skills
    imagination creativity skills, 19, 22–23, 46, 90–91
    innovation creativity skills, 19, 23–24
Crockett, L., 13
curricular goals. *See also* goals
    designing problems-first projects and, 119, 121
    example for English language arts, 134
    example for science class, 129
    example for social studies class, 138
curriculum, expanding your view of.
    See multisubject approach
curriculum as a problem to be solved, 30–32
curriculum drives assessment idea, 100

D

Darling-Hammond, L., 8
data
    information investigation skills and, 20
    problems of unreliable data, 79–80

debriefing (four Ds of problem solving), 27, 66–67. *See also* four Ds of problem solving

Deci, E., 106

defining (four Ds of problem solving). *See also* four Ds of problem solving
- about, 56–57
- correctness of definitions, 58
- definitions of the problem, 57
- focus and, 58–59
- independent problem-solving skills and, 27

designing (four Ds of problem solving). *See also* four Ds of problem solving
- about, 59, 61
- generating ideas and, 61
- independent problem-solving skills and, 27
- knowledge and expertise and, 62–63
- resources and, 63
- solution design form, 60
- solution overview and, 61–62
- time management and, 63–64

designing problems-first projects
- assessments and, 124–125
- double-mindedness and, 119, 121
- problem-givers and, 123
- problem-solvers and, 122–123
- problems and, 123–124
- problems-first project planning flowchart, 120
- products and, 121–122

digital generation, needs and a new approach for
- keys to a new approach. *See* keys to a new approach
- new needs of a changing generation, the. *See* needs of a changing generation
- thinking and processing skills students need for the future. *See* thinking and processing skills

divergent thinking
- convergent thinking and, 97
- creative nonfiction and, 91
- definition of, 95
- Idea-Storm Think Tank and, 95
- imagination creativity skills and, 22
- independent problem-solving skills and, 27
- information synthesis and, 82
- innovation creativity skills and, 24
- three-dimensional thinking and, 17–18
- writing process and, 93

doing (four Ds of problem solving), 27, 64–66. *See also* four Ds of problem solving

Dragnet teaching, 77–78

E

easing yourself out of the picture. *See* teachers, easing yourself out of the picture

Ebbinghaus, H., 11

educating the whole mind
- about, 89
- conclusion, 98
- fact-based imagination and, 90–91
- Idea-Storm Think Tank and, 94–98
- questions for discussion, 98
- writing process and, 92–94

Einstein, A., 78, 96

ensuring problems first and teaching second. *See* problems first and teaching second

envisioning a new role for the teacher. *See* teachers, role of in problems-first approach

equipping students with the four Ds of problem solving. *See* four Ds of problem solving

establishing a real-world link using role-play. *See* role-playing

evaluating holistically. *See* assessments

evaluating the students' level of thought. *See* thinking, levels of

examples of problems-first lesson plans
- about, 129
- conclusion, 144–145
- junior high school science class example, 129–133
- junior high school social studies class example, 138–144
- middle school English language arts class example, 134–138
- problems-first learning approach and, 45
- questions for discussion, 145

expanding your view of the curriculum. *See* multisubject approach

F

fact retrieval approach, 77–78

feedback
- formative assessments and rubrics and, 107
- peer assessments and, 105

forgetting curve, 11

formative assessments. *See also* assessments
- rubrics and, 107–108
- short analysis assessments and, 102

four Ds of problem solving. *See also* problem solving
- about, 2, 55–56
- conclusion, 68–69
- debriefing, 66–67

defining, 56–59
designing, 59–64
doing, 64–66
independent problem-solving skills and, 27
problems-first teaching and, 118–119
questions for discussion, 69
Future of Jobs (World Economic Forum), 15

G

goals. *See also* curricular goals
of complex problem-solving, 125–126
for English language arts class example, 134
for science class example, 129–130
for social studies class example, 138–139
graphic design, 22, 93

H

Hattie, J., 20
higher-level thinking. *See also* thinking, levels of
creative nonfiction and, 91
elements of, 78–79
example of, 84–86
information evaluation and, 83
problems-first instructional approach and, 2

I

ideas
generating ideas, 61, 95–97
innovation creativity skills and, 23
Idea-Storm Think Tank
about, 94–95
convergent thinking and, 97–98
generating ideas and, 95–97
imagination creativity skills
fact-based imagination and, 90–91
problems-first approach and, 46
seven pillars of success and, 19, 22–23
incremental change, 118
independence. *See* autonomy
independent problem-solving skills, 19, 26–28
information, scrutinizing, 81–82
information analysis, steps of, 80–82
information investigation skills, 19, 20–21
information synthesis, aspects of, 82–83
innovation creativity skills, 19, 23–24
interdependent collaboration skills, 19, 25–26
intermediate deadlines, 64
internal attitude skills
problems-first approach and, 46

self-assessment and, 108–110
seven pillars of success and, 19–20
interpersonal skills, 19, 24–25
interviewing/questioning abilities
four Ds of problem solving and, 57, 62
problems to independence progression and, 31
role-playing and, 49, 50
introduction, 1–4

J

job skills for the world of work, 15
Jukes, I., 13

K

keys to a new approach
about, 29–30
authentic teaching and assessment and, 32–34
conclusion, 35
curriculum as a problem to be solved and, 30–32
questions for discussion, 35
Krathwohl, D., 78, 79

L

learning how to create problems-first projects
about, 37
easing yourself out of the picture. *See* teachers, easing yourself out of the picture
educating the whole mind. *See* educating the whole mind
ensuring that problems are first and teaching is second. *See* problems first and teaching second
envisioning a new role for the teacher. *See* teachers, role of in problems-first approach
equipping students with the four Ds of problem solving. *See* four Ds of problem solving
establishing a real-world link using role-play. *See* role-playing
evaluating holistically. *See* assessments
evaluating the students' level of thought. *See* thinking, levels of
expanding your view of the curriculum. *See* multisubject approach
lesson plans
about, 129
conclusion, 144–145

junior high school science class example, 129–133
junior high school social studies class example, 138–144
middle school English language arts class example, 134–138
questions for discussion, 145

M

making the shift to problems-first teaching
    examples of problems-first lesson plans. *See* examples of problems-first lesson plans; lesson plans
    pointers for shifting to a problems-first approach. *See* shifting to a problems-first approach

Maxwell, J., 95
McCain, T., 13
memorization
    assessments and, 107
    teaching as telling, learning as listening and, 11
    thinking and processing skills and, 15–16
metacognition
    independent problem-solving skills and, 27
    internal attitude skills and, 20
    three-dimensional thinking and, 17–18
mindset of education, 8
Montessori method, xiii
multisubject approach. *See also* subject areas
    about, 71
    alternatives to compartmentalizing and, 71–72
    common ground and, 74
    conclusion, 74–75
    example for, 73
    open-ended problems with unknown possibilities and, 72
    questions for discussion, 75
    reaching out and, 74
Myth of the Muse, The (Reeves and Reeves), 22

N

needs and a new approach for a digital generation
    keys to a new approach. *See* keys to a new approach
    new needs of a changing generation, the. *See* needs of a changing generation
    thinking and processing skill students need for the future. *See* thinking and processing skills

needs of a changing generation
    about, 7
    conclusion, 14
    problems for students, 11–13
    questions for discussion, 14
    situation in schools, 8–11

O

one-minute essays, 103
ownership of learning/problems, xiii, 32, 47, 49, 50

P

PBL (project-based learning), 16–17, 27
peer assessments, 105. *See also* assessments
performance assessments, 101, 102. *See also* assessments
planned backward approach, 34
platoon schools, 8
PLC (professional learning communities), 74
poorly principle, 119
portfolios as assessments, 103–105. *See also* assessments
problem, the
    designing problems-first projects, 123–124
    example for English language arts class, 135
    example for science class, 130–131
    example for social studies class, 140
problem-givers
    designing problems-first projects and, 123
    example for English language arts class, 135
    example for science class, 130
    example for social studies class, 139
problem-solvers
    designing problems-first projects and, 122–123
    example for English language arts class, 135
    example for science class, 130
    example for social studies class, 139
problem solving. *See also* four Ds of problem solving
    complex problem-solving, 26, 125–126
    goal of, 125–126
    independent problem-solving skills, 19, 26–28
problems first and teaching second
    about, 43–44
    benefits of, 46–47
    conclusion, 47–48
    questions for discussion, 48
    what the approach looks like, 44, 46

problems-first instructional approach
    about, 2
    benefits of, 46–47
    examples of a problems-first lesson, 45
    keys to a new approach. *See* keys to a new approach
    role of the teacher in problems-first approach. *See* teachers, role of in problems-first approach
    shifting to problems-first teaching. *See* shifting to a problems-first approach
    solving the problem, 47
    what the problems-first approach looks like, 44–46
problems-first projects
    designing problems-first projects. *See* designing problems-first projects
    learning how to create problems-first projects. *See* learning how to create problems-first projects
problems to independence progression, 30–31
process skills, 13, 16. *See also* thinking and processing skills
product, the
    designing problems-first projects and, 121–122
    example for English language arts class, 134
    example for science class, 130
    example for social studies class, 139
professional learning communities (PLC), 74
project-based learning (PBL), 16–17, 27
projects, designing. *See* designing problems-first projects
projects per term, 126
prompts and short analysis assessments, 103

Q

questioning. *See* interviewing/questioning abilities

R

real-world links. *See also* role-playing
    problems-first instructional approach and, 43
    project-based learning and, 16
    role-playing and, 49–50
Reeves, B., 22
Reeves, D., 22
Right to Learn, The (Darling-Hammond), 8
role-playing. *See also* problem-givers; problem-solvers
    about, 49

    benefits of, 49–50
    conclusion, 53
    example of, 51–52
    problems-first approach and, 44
    questions for discussion, 53
    starting small, 52–53
rubrics, 107–108, 124
Ryan, R., 106

S

school skills, 2
self-assessment. *See also* assessments
    internal attitude skills and, 20, 108–110
    portfolios as assessments and, 103
    types of assessments/authentic assessments, 105–106
seven pillars of success
    example for English language arts class, 134
    example for science class, 130
    example for social studies class, 138–139
    imagination creativity skills and, 19, 22–23
    independent problem-solving skills and, 19, 26–28
    information investigation skills and, 19, 20–21
    innovation creativity skills and, 19, 23–24
    interdependent collaboration skills and, 19, 25–26
    internal attitude skills and, 19–20
    interpersonal skills and, 19, 24–25
    problems-first approach and, 46
    problems-first projects and, 121
Shaffer, P., 90
shifting to a problems-first approach
    about, 117
    conclusion, 127
    designing problems-first projects and, 119–125
    goal of complex problem-solving and, 125–126
    projects per term and, 126
    questions for discussion, 127
    things to remember when beginning problems-first teaching and, 117–119
short analysis assessments, 101–103. *See also* assessments
skills. *See also* communication skills; creativity skills; seven pillars of success; thinking and processing skills
    job skills for the world of work, 15

process skills, 16
school skills, 2
sponge assessments, 100. *See also* assessments
Stanford University, 74
sticky voting, 97
subject areas, 40. *See also* multisubject approach

T

task lists, 63–64
teachers
    conclusion, 112
    crafters of problems, 40
    creators of engagement, 40
    multisubject approach and, 74
    questions for discussion, 113
teachers, easing yourself out of the picture
    about, 111–112
    conclusion, 112
    questions for discussion, 113
teachers, role of in problems-first approach
    about, 39
    conclusion, 41
    critical new role and, 39–40
    goals for every subject area and, 40
    questions for discussion, 41
    response to resistance and, 41
teaching. *See also* problems first and teaching second
    authentic teaching and assessment, 32–34
    pointers for shifting to a problems-first approach. *See* shifting to a problems-first approach
    teaching as facilitating, learning as discovery method, 30
    teaching as telling, learning as listening, 9, 10, 11–13
teamwork, 25–26
technology
    interpersonal skills and, 24–25
    problems for students and, 13
    in schools, 3
thinking, levels of
    about, 77–78
    conclusion, 87
    elements of higher-level thinking, 78–79
    example of, 84–86
    information analysis and, 80–82
    information evaluation and, 83–84
    information synthesis and, 82–83
    questions for discussion, 87
    role-playing and, 49, 50
    unreliable data and, 79–80
    visual representations of thinking, 103
thinking and processing skills
    about, 15–17
    conclusion, 28
    questions for discussion, 28
    seven pillars of success and, 19–28
    three-dimensional thinking, 17–18
three-dimensional thinking, 17–18, 27
time management, 63–64

U

understanding new needs and a new approach for a digital generation
    keys to a new approach. *See* keys to a new approach
    new needs of a changing generation, the. *See* needs of a changing generation
    thinking and processing skill students need for the future. *See* thinking and processing skills
Understanding the Digital Generation (Jukes, McCain, and Crockett), 13

V

velcro learning, 31–32
visual representations of thinking, 103

W

Wang, J., 105
whole mind, educating the. *See* educating the whole mind
Wiggins, G., 32–33, 34, 107–108
Wiliam, D., 102
Wirt, W., 8
World Economic Forum, 15
writing process, 22, 92–94
Wurman, R., 31–32

Learning Without Classrooms
Frank Kelly and Ted McCain
Learning Without Classrooms outlines new guidelines for how schools must operate to remain relevant and effective as we move further into the 21st century. The authors detail six crucial elements of schooling and how to address them concurrently to improve secondary schools.
BKF820

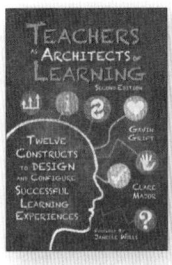
Teachers as Architects of Learning (Second Edition)
Gavin Grift and Clare Major
Craft a personal blueprint for teaching that ensures student learning stands as the foundation of your classroom. Drawing on research from the field and the authors' professional experience, this resource guides educators in building their wisdom around the art of teaching.
BKB010

Ambitious Instruction
Brad Cawn
Discover a blueprint for making rigor visible, accessible, and actionable in grade 6–12 classrooms. *Ambitious Instruction* guides readers toward using the twin tenets of problem-based learning and synthesis to significantly strengthen students' ability to read, write, and think within and across disciplines.
BKF842

Ready for Anything
Suzette Lovely
Effective teaching and learning must reflect what's happening technologically, socially, economically, and globally. In *Ready for Anything*, author Suzette Lovely introduces four touchstones that will invigorate students' curiosity and aspirations and prepare them for college, careers, and life in the 21st century.
BKF848

Solution Tree | Press
a division of
Solution Tree

Visit SolutionTree.com or call 800.733.6786 to order.

Wait! Your professional development journey doesn't have to end with the last pages of this book.

We realize improving student learning doesn't happen overnight. And your school or district shouldn't be left to puzzle out all the details of this process alone.

No matter where you are on the journey, we're committed to helping you get to the next stage.

Take advantage of everything from **custom workshops** to **keynote presentations** and **interactive web and video conferencing**. We can even help you develop an action plan tailored to fit your specific needs.

Let's get the conversation started.

Call 888.763.9045 today.

SolutionTree.com